HOT spot 2

Colin Granger

Student's Book

Contents

1 Wayne's world

❶ Picture search

1.01 Find these in the pictures:

| bike   sea   Labrador   pier   flat   football boots |

❷ Presentation

a) *1.02* Listen and read. Look at the pictures to help you understand.

1

Hi. My name's Wayne Turner. I'm twelve years old. And this is my world!
This is my home. My address is Flat 8, 19 Marina Road, Brighton. Our flat isn't big, but the view is fantastic! Look. You can see my hometown Brighton, the sea and the pier. Brighton isn't a big town, but it's famous. Every year a lot of people come here for a day by the sea.

2

That's my sister, Tina. She's sixteen. And that's our dog, Bobby. He's a Labrador and he's very friendly. Today's the best day of the year. Can you guess why? Yes, it's the 15th of September – my birthday! And these are two of my favourite things: my bike and my football boots. My boots are a bit muddy at the moment and they aren't new, but they're great! My mum says I'm sports mad. My top three sports are football, basketball and athletics.

b) *1.02* Listen again. Look at the pictures and point to the things Wayne talks about.

Real English

fantastic   the best
a bit   sports mad

❸ Comprehension

a) Read the text again. Find the answers to these questions.

1 What's Wayne's surname?
2 How old is he?
3 What's his address?
4 Who's Tina?
5 When's Wayne's birthday?
6 What are his favourite things?
7 What are his top three sports?

b) ⟨1.03⟩ Listen and check.

c) Then work with a classmate. Ask and answer.

What's Wayne's surname?   Turner.

❹ Grammar practice

Verb *be*

Complete with '*m, is*, '*s, are* '*re*.

1 I____ 12 years old.
2 Wayne's flat ____n't big. It____ small.
3 Tina ____n't twelve. She____ sixteen.
4 Wayne and Tina ____n't cousins.
   They____ brother and sister.
5 Wayne's football boots ____ a bit muddy and
   they ____n't new, but they____ really great.

👀 Grammar page 94

❺ Ordinal numbers

a) ⟨1.04⟩ Listen and practise saying the numbers.

1st first	9th ninth	17th seventeenth
2nd second	10th tenth	18th eighteenth
3rd third	11th eleventh	19th nineteenth
4th fourth	12th twelfth	20th twentieth
5th fifth	13th thirteenth	21st twenty-first
6th sixth	14th fourteenth	22nd twenty-second, etc.
7th seventh	15th fifteenth	30th thirtieth
8th eighth	16th sixteenth	31st thirty-first, etc.

b) Work with two or three classmates. Find out when their birthdays are.

When's your birthday?

It's on the 21st of March.

Writing tip

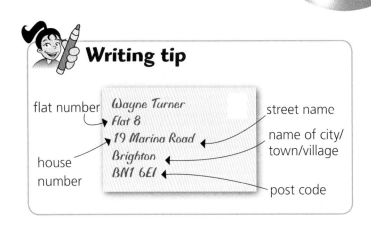

flat number — Wayne Turner
Flat 8
19 Marina Road — street name
Brighton — name of city/town/village
BN1 6EI — post code
house number
street name
name of city/town/village
post code

My English file

Write about your world. Use the text in Activity 2 as a model.

Hi. My name's Ewa Springer. I'm twelve years old. And this is my world! My address is . . .

❻ Check your English

a) Work with a classmate. Ask and answer these questions.

What's your surname?   Linden.

1 What's your surname?
2 How old are you?
3 What's your address?
4 When's your birthday?
5 What are your favourite things?
6 What are your top three sports?

b) Play the Speed Game. Go round the class. Say what number you are.

I'm second.
I'm first.
I'm third.
I'm...

Lesson objectives
• Describing people's appearance
• Comparing people's interests

2 Mary's mate Polly

❶ Presentation

a) (1.05) Listen and read. Look at the pictures to help you understand.

My mate Polly

I like music, Polly likes sport.

My hair's long, her hair's short.

I'm always late, Polly's always early.

I've got straight hair, her hair's curly.

I've got dogs, Polly's got cats.

I'm good at Art, she's good at Maths.

I'm quite short and Polly's quite tall.

I play hip hop, she plays football.

I wear trainers and she wears shoes.

I watch soaps, she watches the news.

I've got brown eyes, her eyes are blue.

My bike's old, her bike's new.

I eat salad, Polly eats cheese.

I say sorry and she says please.

I can water-ski, Polly can skate.

We're very different, but she's still a good mate.

Polly

Mary

b) (1.06) Listen again. Then repeat the poem with your classmates.

Remember!

Short form	Full form
I'm	I am
He/She's	He/She is
We're	We are
I've got	I have got
He/She's got	He/She has got

Grammar spot
be, have got, present simple, can

Be: Her eyes **are** blue.
Have got: I **'ve got** brown eyes.
Present simple: I **play** hip hop, she **plays** football.
Can: I **can** water-ski, she **can** skate.

👀 Grammar Verb *be*, page 94; *Have got*, page 94; *Present simple*, page 95; *Can*, page 96

❷ Comprehension

Work in small teams. Take it in turns to close your books. Ask and answer about *Mary* or *Polly*.

Who likes sport?   Polly.

1   Who likes sport?
2   Who's always early?
3   Who's good at Maths?
4   Who plays football?
5   Who watches soaps?
6   Who's got blue eyes?
7   Who's got an old bike?
8   Who can skate?

❸ Listening

a) *1.06* Look at Mary's classmates. Listen and match the descriptions with the names. Use the chart below to help you.

Frank   **Billy**   **Sean**   **Jake**

b) *1.07* Listen and check.

c) Now describe the boys with *He's got … His hair is … It's … and …*

He's got blue eyes. His hair is brown. It's medium length and curly.

Hair:

brown   dark brown   black

blonde   grey   red

curly   wavy   straight

Eye colour:

green   blue   brown

My English file

Write a description about you and a friend. Use:

I'm … and he/she's …
I've got … and he/she's got …
I like/play/wear/watch/eat… and he/she likes/ plays/wears/watches/eats …
I can … and he/she can …

I'm quite tall and he's quite short. I've got black hair and he's got blonde hair. I eat…

❹ Pronunciation

a) Match the words in A with a word that rhymes in B.

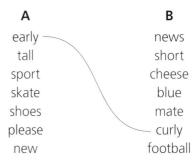

A	B
early	news
tall	short
sport	cheese
skate	blue
shoes	mate
please	curly
new	football

b) *1.08* Listen and check. Practise saying the words.

❺ Check your English

a) Complete the sentences about Mary with *is*, *has got*, *can*, *plays*.

1   Mary _____ hip hop.
2   She _____ good at Art.
3   She _____ water-ski.
4   She _____ long, straight hair.

b) Choose the correct words in the description of this girl.

1   She's got *green/brown eyes*.

2   Her hair is *dark/light* brown.

3   It's *short/long* and *curly/ straight*.

Lesson objectives
• Giving personal information
• Talking about likes and dislikes

3 The other side of the world

❶ Picture search

(1.09) Match these words with the pictures.

Shetland – f

> Shetland   sailing   meat   keyboards
> carrots   New Zealand   ears   hanging out
> purple   getting up early   music   tests

❷ Presentation

a) (1.10) Ian and Nyree are e-pals.
Look at the pictures and listen.

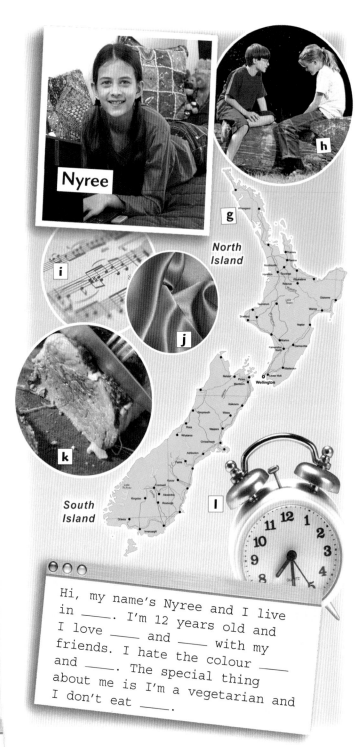

Nyree

North Island

South Island

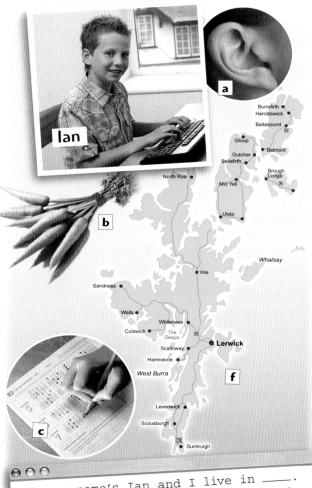

Ian

Hi, my name's Nyree and I live
in ____. I'm 12 years old and
I love ____ and ____ with my
friends. I hate the colour ____
and ____. The special thing
about me is I'm a vegetarian and
I don't eat ____.

Hi, my name's Ian and I live in ____.
I'm 11 years old and I like ____ and
playing the ____. I don't like revising
for ____ and I don't like ____. The
special thing about me is I can wiggle
my ____. Can you do that?

b) (1.10) Listen again. Then fill in the missing words.

Grammar spot
Like/don't like/love/hate

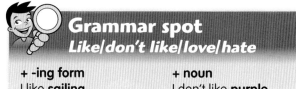

+ -ing form	+ noun
I like **sailing**.	I don't like **purple**.
I hate **getting up** early.	I love **music**.

❸ Comprehension

a) Work with a classmate. Choose to be Ian or Nyree. Ask and answer the questions.

> What's your name?   Ian

> What's your name?

1 What's your name?
2 Where do you live?
3 How old are you?
4 What do you like?
5 What don't you like?

b) Now ask and answer about you.

❹ Writing and speaking

a) Copy and complete this table.

	love	like	don't like	hate
tidying my room				✓
watching TV		✓		
spaghetti				
yellow				
playing games				
shopping				
reading				
Mondays				

b) Tell your classmates your likes and dislikes.

> I hate tidying my room. I like watching TV. ...

My English file

Write an e-pal letter about you. Use Ian's and Nyree's emails as models.

Hi, my name's Sophie and I live in Russia. I'm twelve years old and I love swimming and volleyball. I don't like looking after my little brother and I don't like watching football. The special thing about me is I can swim two kilometres.

❺ Reading

a) Are the sentences true about you? Answer with T (= true) or F (= false).

1 F

1 I can do cartwheels.
2 I don't like sweets and chocolate.
3 I live with my grandmother.
4 I've got six sisters.
5 I like doing homework.

b) Write five special things about you.

I can wiggle my ears.
I can stand on one leg ...

c) Then work in a small group. Read your sentences to your classmates.

❻ Song 🎵

1.11 Find the song *All about me* on page 90.

❼ Check your English

a) Write four true sentences about you with:

1 I like playing football.
1 I like …   3 I love …
2 I don't like …   4 I hate …

b) Write three questions to ask a classmate with:

1 Do you like playing computer games?
1 Do you like …?
2 Do you love …?
3 Do you hate …?

c) Then ask and answer your questions.

> Do you like playing computer games?

> Yes, I do.

4 My country

❶ Reading

a) *1.12* Listen and read. Where is Tim from?

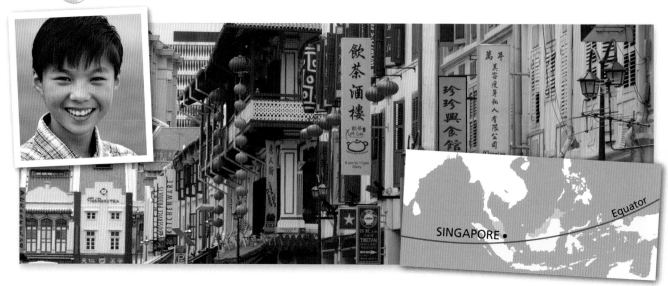

SINGAPORE • Equator

Tim lives in Singapore in Southeast Asia. He lives with his parents and sister in a flat on the 22nd floor of a **high-rise building**. Many Singaporeans live in flats.

Singapore is very close to the Equator and the weather is always hot and humid. But it's cool inside Tim's home because his family has got **air-conditioning**.

There are four official languages in Singapore: English, **Mandarin Chinese**, Malay and Tamil. Tim speaks two languages: he speaks English at school and Mandarin at home with his parents.

Tim's favourite food is noodles with meat and vegetables. Tim and his family don't eat with a **knife and fork**, they use **chopsticks**.

Tim's favourite sports are tennis, basketball, football and **water sports**.

b) Read again. Match the pictures with the words in the text.

1 high-rise building

❷ Speaking

a) (1.13) Listen and practise asking the questions. Think about the answers.

1 Where does Tim live?
2 What's the weather like in Singapore?
3 What language does Tim speak at school?
4 What's Tim's favourite food?
5 What are his favourite sports?

b) Work with a classmate. Ask and answer the questions.

> Where does Tim live?

> He lives in Singapore.

c) (1.14) Now listen and check.

Fun spot

Mr. X

a) (1.16) Work with a classmate. Listen to the description of Mr X then find him in the picture. Don't call out the answer.

b) (1.16) Listen again. Are you right?

❸ Listening

a) (1.15) Listen. Which subjects does Nyree talk about?

> Where she lives   The weather
> Languages   Food   Sport

b) (1.15) Listen again. Are these sentences true or false?

1 Nyree lives on New Zealand's South Island.
2 Her mum and dad speak Maori.
3 Nyree learns Maori at school.
4 Nyree's favourite sport is tennis.
5 A lot of New Zealanders like playing cricket and football.

❹ Writing

Write about your country. Begin with *I live in … in …*

I live in Geneva in Switzerland. There are four official languages in my country: French, German, Italian and Romansch. I speak French and I learn German and English . . .

Review

Check you can do these things.

1 I can ask and give information with the verb be.

a) Complete these questions with 's or *are*.

1 What _____ your surname?
2 How old _____ you?
3 What _____ your address?

4 What _____ the date today?
5 What _____ your top three sports?
6 When _____ you birthday?

b) Then use the questions to give information about yourself.

My surname is Kobler. I'm twelve years old. My address is …

c) Write three sentences giving information about your best friend.

His surname is …

2 I can say this poem. Use the pictures and initial letters to help you.

I like music, Polly likes sport, …

I like , Polly likes sport.

My hair's long, her hair's s_____.

I'm always l_____, Polly's always early.

I've got straight hair, her hair's .

I've got dogs, Polly's got cats.

I'm good at Art, she's good at

I'm quite s_____ and Polly's is quite tall.

I play hip hop, she plays f_____.

I wear and she wears shoes.

I watch soaps, she watches the n_____.

I've got b_____ eyes, her eyes are blue.

My bike's old, her bike's new.

I eat , Polly eats cheese.

I say sorry and she says p_____.

I can water-ski, Polly can

We're very d_____, but she's still a good mate.

3 I can use the *present simple* to describe people's lifestyles and interests.

a) Make true sentences about you with these verbs:

I like … I play … I wear … I watch … I eat …

I like sweets. I play …

b) Then make true sentences about a good friend with the same verbs.

Maria likes computer games. She plays …

4 I can describe people's appearance.

Describe these children's hair and eyes.

1   She's got green eyes. Her hair is...

5 I can talk about the things I like and don't like.

a) Look at the pictures and ask your classmate questions with *Do you like/love/hate ...?*

Do you like swimming?   Yes, I do.

1 swimming

2 playing games

3 running

4 doing homework

5 tidying your room

6 getting up early

b) Now make true sentences about you with: *I like/don't like/love/hate ...*

I don't like swimming.

6 I can understand a text giving information about a different country.

Hello, my name's Anna and I live in Reykjavik in Iceland. Iceland is an island in the North Atlantic Ocean. Icelanders eat a lot of fish and the most popular sports are football, handball, basketball and athletics. The official language of Iceland is Icelandic, but most Icelanders can also speak English.

Are these sentences true or false?

1   Reykjavik is the name of a country.
2   Iceland is an island.
3   Icelanders don't like fish.
4   Icelanders speak Icelandic.

Extra special

USA Quiz

1 These are all American cities. Which one is the capital?

A New York

B Washington DC

C Los Angeles

2 What is this popular American sport called?

A American football

B Basketball

C Baseball

3 This is where the President of the United States lives. What is the name of this building?

A The White House

B The Empire State Building

C The Pentagon

4 What is this place famous for?

A Computers

B Films

C Sport

5 Where is this American flag?

A On a mountain

B In a city

C On the moon

6 There are 50 states in America. Which three of these places are American states?

A Mexico

B Texas

C Cuba

D California

E Canada

F Brazil

G Florida

H Argentina

USA

7 Can you match these British English and American English words?

1) biscuit
2) rubbish
3) mobile phone
4) trousers
5) trainers
6) rubber

a) cellphone
b) pants
c) cookie
d) eraser
e) trash
f) sneakers

8 What is this statue called?

A   The Statue of Liberty
B   The Statue of Happiness
C   The Statue of Light.

Extra Activity

Write a similar quiz about your country.

Mini project

1 Read Liz's poster. Are any of her loves and hates the same as yours?

My loves and hates

loves

1 I love hanging out with my friends.
2 I love watching TV.
3 I love playing with my sister.
4 I love swimming.
5 I love my grandmother.

hates

1 I hate getting up early.
2 I hate spinach.
3 I hate tests.
4 I hate going for walks.
5 I hate tidying my room.

Liz

2 Make a poster about your loves and hates.

3 Compare your poster with a classmate. How many of your loves and hates are the same?

5 Saturday morning chores

1 Picture search

Look at the list. Find the chores in the picture.

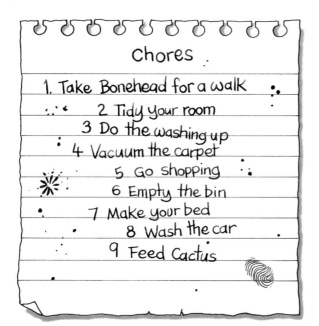

Chores

1. Take Bonehead for a walk
2. Tidy your room
3. Do the washing up
4. Vacuum the carpet
5. Go shopping
6. Empty the bin
7. Make your bed
8. Wash the car
9. Feed Cactus

2 Presentation

a) *1.17* Look at the picture and listen. What are the Glooms doing?

Sam and Pam

Gordon & Vera

Rudolph

Helga

Bernard

Mandy

Cynthia

Martha

Vincent

b) *1.17* Listen again. Have you got similar chores?

Grammar spot
Present continuous

Mandy **is taking** the dog for a walk.
Gordon and Vera **are making** the bed.

Grammar page 96

18

❸ Grammar practice

Look at the picture in Activity 2. Make sentences about what the Glooms are doing.

> wash   empty   take   go   make
> do   vacuum   feed   tidy

1   Sam and Pam are tidying their room.
2   Mandy's taking Bonehead for a walk.

1   Sam and Pam _____ their room.
2   Mandy_____ Bonehead for a walk.
3   Martha _____ the bin.
4   Bernard _____ the car.
5   Gordon and Vera _____ the bed.
6   Vincent _____ shopping.
7   Cynthia _____ the carpet.
8   Rudolph _____ the washing up.
9   Helga _____ Cactus.

❹ Speaking

a) Find these things in the picture in Activity 2.

raincoat   rubber gloves   toothbrush

fish   roller skates   toys

b) 1.18 Listen to the questions. Think about the answers.

1   What's Bernard washing with his toothbrush?
2   What are Sam and Pam putting under the rug?
3   What's Cactus eating?
4   What's Martha wearing on her hands?
5   What's Rudolph wearing?
6   What's Vincent wearing on his feet?

c) Work with a classmate. Ask and answer.

> What's Bernard washing with his tootbrush?

> His car.

❺ Class survey: chores

a) Work with two or three classmates. Write a list of chores.

Look after my little brother/sister
Wash the clothes

b) Find out how many of your classmates do these chores. Write the results on the board.

❻ Listening

a) 1.19 Listen. Then match the sentences with the pictures.

> He's having a shower.   She's closing the window.
> They're riding their bikes.   They're cleaning their teeth.
> She's brushing her hair.   He's opening the door.

1   She's brushing her hair.

b) Then work with a classmate. Ask and answer about the pictures with:

What's he/she doing? | What are they doing?
He's/She's/They're … …

> What's she doing?

> She's brushing her hair.

❼ Check your English

a) Complete with the present continuous of the verb in brackets.

A: What _____ you _____? (do)
B: I _____ my room. (tidy)

A: Where _____ she _____? (go)
B: She _____ to school. (go)

b) Look at the picture in Activity 2. Write three questions to ask your classmates with *What's …?* Then close your books and take it in turns to ask and answer.

> What's Cynthia vacuuming?

> The carpet.

6 Work and play

❶ Presentation

a) *1.20* Listen and read.

SURVEY   How often do you ...?

WORK

1 tidy your room

2 do the washing up

3 go food shopping

4 lay the table

PLAY

5 go swimming

6 play computer games

7 surf the Internet

8 hang out with friends

b) *1.21* Now listen to Ian and complete the sentences with the words from the box.

*1   He tidies his room **once** or **twice** a week.*

| once twice three four every never |
| morning day Sunday week weekend month |

1   He tidies his room _____ or _____ a _____.
2   He does the washing up _____ or_____ times a _____.
3   He _____ shopping.
4   He lays the table for dinner every _____.
5   He goes swimming _____ Saturday _____.
6   He plays computer games every _____.
7   He surfs the Internet _____ day.
8   He hangs out with his friends _____ day after school.

c) *1.21* Listen again and check.

Grammar spot
Expressions of frequency

How often does he tidy his room?
He tidies his room **once or twice a week**.

How often does he go food shopping?
He goes shopping **every Saturday morning**.

(👓 Grammar page 97)

❷ Speaking and writing

a) Complete the survey about you. Don't show your classmates.

1 twice a week, 2 every weekend, 3 every morning. 4 never ...

b) Work with a classmate. Ask and answer.

> How often do you tidy your room?

> I tidy my room twice a week.

c) Write three true sentences about your classmate.

She plays computer games every evening. She goes swimming...

❸ Grammar Practice

Adverbs of frequency

a) Write five sentences about what you do after school with:

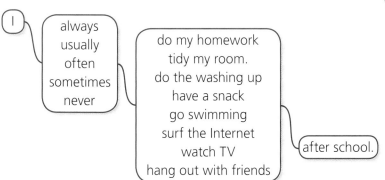

I	always usually often sometimes never	do my homework tidy my room. do the washing up have a snack go swimming surf the Internet watch TV hang out with friends	after school.

1 I always do the washing up after school.
2 I usually hang out with my friends after school.
3 ...

b) Tell a classmate how often you do things after school.

> I sometimes go swimming after school.

❹ Writing

a) Write three questions to ask a classmate with *How often*.

1   How often do you walk to school?

b) Exchange questions. Then write answers to your classmate's questions. Use expressions of frequency.

1   How often do you walk to school? Every day.

My English file

Write three more sentences about Tidy Ted.

Ted always does his homework. He does the washing up every day. He never makes a mess...

❺ Song 🎵

(1.22) Find the song *Rock star* on page 90.

❻ Check your English

a) (1.23) Listen. Find out what Nyree does:

> once or twice a week
> always   sometimes   often
> every Saturday afternoon
> three or four times a week

b) (1.23) Listen again. All these sentences are false. Correct them.

1   Nyree sometimes tidies her room.
2   She never looks after her little sister.
3   She does the washing up every day.
4   She goes swimming three or four times a month.
5   She goes to the cinema every day.
6   She sometimes hangs out with her friends after school.

7 Saving the world

❶ Picture search

(1.24) Find these things in the pictures.

| plastic bottles   metal cans   glass jars |
| paper   cardboard boxes   lorry   rubbish |

❷ Presentation

a) (1.25) Listen and read. What are the people in the pictures doing?

Recycle!

1 We don't throw away rubbish at our school. We recycle it and put the rubbish into the correct recycling box.

2 This bottle's made of plastic and I'm recycling it. I'm putting it into the yellow recycling box.

3 I'm not throwing these cans away. They're made of metal and I'm putting them into the blue recycling box.

4 We all recycle at our school. This is our school secretary and she's putting the old paper into the green recycling box.

5 And that's our school cook. Those jars and bottles are made of glass and he's recycling them. That box is made of cardboard. We collect all cardboard boxes at our school and recycle them.

A big lorry comes to the school every Friday and collects all our paper, cardboard, glass, metal and plastic for recycling.

b) (1.25) Listen again. Do you recycle at school?

❸ Comprehension

Look at the pictures in Activity 2. Answer the questions.

1 What are the children holding in picture 1?
2 What's the bottle made of in picture 2?
3 Is the girl throwing away the cans in picture 3?
4 Where is the secretary putting the paper?
5 Is the cook recycling the glass?
6 How often does the lorry come to the school?

Grammar spot
It/them

This **bottle's** made of plastic. I'm recycling **it**.

Those **jars** are made of glass and he's recycling **them**.

Grammar page 99

❹ Speaking

a) Work with your classmate. Ask and answer.

What's the bottle made of?

It's made of glass.

What are the wrappers made of?

They're made of ...

1 **bottle**   2 **wrappers**   3 **can**

4 **packet**   5 **pots**   6 **jar**

b) 🔊 *1.26* Listen and check.

c) Now match the things with the correct recycling box. Ask and answer.

Where does the bottle go?

It goes in the green box.

Where do the wrappers go?

 Cardboard

 metal

 glass

 paper

 plastic

Grammar spot
Present simple/ present continuous

Present simple
We always **recycle** rubbish.
We **collect** all cardboard boxes.

Present continuous
I'm **recycling** this bottle.
She's **putting** the paper into the green recycling box.

👓 Grammar page 98

❺ Grammar practice

a) Look at this girl's room. What can you see?

1　She plays *tennis/football*.
2　She likes *sweets/chocolate*.
3　She goes *swimming/ice-skating*.
4　She wears *jeans/skirts*.
5　She reads *books/magazines*.

b) Look at the picture again. What's she doing? Which three sentences are correct?

1　She's playing football.
2　She's eating a chocolate bar.
3　She's ice-skating.
4　She's wearing jeans.
5　She's reading a book.

❻ Check your English

a) Are these sentences about you true or false?

1　I often eat chocolate.
2　I'm eating a bar of chocolate.
3　I usually wear jeans.
4　I'm wearing jeans.

b) Find something in the classroom made of:

1 glass   2 plastic   3 cardboard   4 metal   5 paper

8 Helping at home

❶ Reading

a) 🔊 1.27 Listen and read. Find out what this sign means.

My home's a B&B or a Bed and Breakfast. A B&B is a house with one or two bedrooms for paying guests. In my house there are five bedrooms: two are for guests and three are for my family. We've also got two bathrooms: one for the guests and the other for us.

Durham, England

Ruth, 13

Billy, 12

1

In the school holidays, my sister Ruth and I help our parents at our B&B. I help my mum make the beds and vacuum the guests' bedrooms. My sister's good at cooking so she helps our dad cook breakfast. Breakfast is very important in a B&B and our guests usually want a full English breakfast with eggs, bacon, sausage, tomatoes, mushrooms and beans. We also help our parents with another important job: talking to the guests and answering their questions.

2

b) Read again, then answer the questions.
1   They live in a B&B.

1   Where do Billy and his family live?
2   What is a B&B?
3   How does Billy help at the B&B?
4   How does Ruth help at the B&B?
5   What are Billy and Ruth doing in Picture 1?
6   Can you name the different kinds of food in Picture 2?

❷ Listening

a) 〔1.28〕 Listen to Adila. How does she help her mother?

Adila, 11,

Dar es Salaam,

Tanzania

b) 〔1.28〕 Listen again. Match these phrases with the pictures.

> fetch water from the well   cooking dinner
> collect wood for the fire   shaking out the rugs
> sweeping the floor

❸ Speaking

Work with two or three classmates. Take it in turns to ask and answer these questions.

> Where do Billy and Ruth live?

> They live in a B&B.

1   Where do Billy and Ruth live?
2   How many bedrooms has their house got?
3   How do Billy and Ruth help their parents?
4   What's a full English breakfast?
5   Where does Adila live?
6   How does Adila help her mum?
7   Why does Adila like going to the well?

❹ Writing

How do you help at home? Write a list of things you do and things you help do. Use Activities 1 and 2 to help you.

> I usually help with the washing up.
> I sometimes look after my little sister.
> I tidy my room.
> I help my dad in the garden.

Fun spot

Word mountain

a) Complete this word mountain.

1 Musical instrument   <u>keyboards</u>

2 Containers   _____ _____

3 Types of hair   ___ ___ ___

4 Sports   ___ ___ ___ ___

5 Materials   ___ ___ ___ ___ ___

6 Chores   ___ ___ ___ ___ ___ ___

skating

bottle   metal   box

skiing   do the washing up

paper   **curly**   plastic

make the bed   surfing

keyboards   cardboard   **glass**

sailing

tidy the room

straight   lay the table

vacuum the carpet

wavy   empty the bin

b) 〔1.29〕 Check your answers.

Review

Check you can do these things.

1 I can talk about what is happening now with the present continuous.

Complete the dialogue with the present continuous of the verbs in brackets.

A: Hi, Kim. What _____ you _____? (do)

B: I _____ TV. (watch)

A: What _____ you _____ ? (watch)

B: A quiz show. _____ you _____ your homework? (do)

A: No, I'm not. I _____ a book. (read)

B: What _____ your brother _____? (do)

A: He _____ computer games. (play)

B: _____ he _____ Magic Mountain? (play)

A: I don't know.

2 I know the names of these eight chores.

What chores are these children doing? Make sentences with *He's/She's/They're* ...

She's laying the table.

3 I can use expressions of frequency.

Make four true sentences about yourself with:

1 every day   **2** once or twice a week   **3** every afternoon   **4** two or three times a month

I watch TV every day.

4 I can use adverbs of frequency.

Write four true sentences about yourself with *always, often, usually, sometimes, never.*

1 I always walk to school.
1 I walk to school.
2 I hang out with my friends after school.
3 I surf the Internet.
4 I get up early

5 I can use the present simple and the present continuous.

Choose the correct words to complete the postcard.

1 write/'m writing	**2** listen/'m listening	**3** come/'m coming	**4** play/'m playing
5 go/'m going	**6** doesn't like/isn't liking	**7** sits/'s sitting	

Hi Eric,
I ¹_____ this postcard on the beach. It's a beautiful day and I ²_____ to music. I ³_____ to the beach every day. I usually ⁴_____ beach football and ⁵_____ swimming in the sea with my dad. My mum ⁶_____ sitting in the sun. She⁷_____ under a beach umbrella now.
See you soon,
Rich

Eric Jones

6 I can say what things are made of.

Make sentences with *It's/They're made of* … Use the initial letters to help you.

It's made of glass.

1 g____
2 c____
3 m____
4  p____
5 p____
6 g____

Extra special

Guess the object

a) 1.30 Listen. Match the descriptions with the pictures.

1 It's made of paper. It's new. It's got a picture on the front. You read it.

2 They're pink and white. You wear them on your feet. They're expensive.

3 It's round. It's made of leather. It's black and white. You can play with it.

4 It's long and thin. It's made of plastic. You can measure and draw lines with it.

5 They're made of wood. They've got four legs. You can sit on them. You can see them in your classroom.

6 They're made of sugar. They're very sweet. They're different colours. Children like them. You can eat them.

7 It's made of metal. It's white, yellow and green. You drink from it.

8 It's made of plastic. It's long and thin. It's blue. You can write with it.

9 It's quite big and heavy. It's made of leather. It's brown. You can carry things in it.

b) Think of something. Don't tell your classmates.

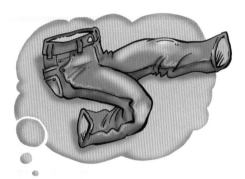

c) Ask and answer to guess the object.

Is it/Are they made of wood/plastic/metal/glass/cardboard/silver/leather/sugar ...?

Is it/Are they big/small/long/short/thick/thin/new/expensive ...?

Is it/Are they black/white/yellow/brown/red/blue/green ...?

Can I see it/them in the classroom/at home/in a shop ... ?

Can I eat/wear/hold/read ... it/them?

Can I play/write ... with it/them?

Are they big?   Yes, they are.

Can I see them in the classroom?

No, you can't.

Can I wear them?   Yes, you can.

Mini project

1 Read about Jasmine's robot. Can you think of some more things Jasmine's robot does?

My Useful Robot

My robot makes breakfast every morning.

She does my Maths homework.

She sings to me every night.

She brings me breakfast in bed on Sunday mornings.

She tidies and cleans my room.

She looks after my little brother.

She eats the food I don't like.

Jasmine

2 Invent a robot and write a description. For example, a sporty robot, an intelligent robot, a funny robot. Illustrate with pictures.

3 Exchange robots with your classmates. Choose the most useful robot.

Lesson objective • Comparing two people or things

9 Friends

Tamsin

Nyree

❶ Picture search

1.31 Listen. Match the words with the pictures in the questionnaire.

talkative – 3

talkative   tall   good at sport   friendly   hard-working   funny

❷ Presentation

a) *1.32* Look at the survey and listen to Nyree.

Friends survey
Compare yourself with a friend.
Choose the correct answer.

1 Are you older than your friend?

★ Yes, I am.
★ No, I'm not.
★ We're the same.

2 Are you better at sport than your friend?

★ Yes, I am.
★ No, I'm not.
★ We're the same.

5 Are you more hard-working than your friend?

★ Yes, I am.
★ No, I'm not.
★ We're the same.

3 Are you more talkative than your friend?

★ Yes, I am.
★ No, I'm not.
★ We're the same.

6 Are you friendlier than your friend?

★ Yes, I am.
★ No, I'm not.
★ We're the same.

4 Are you funnier than your friend?

★ Yes, I am.
★ No, I'm not.
★ We're the same.

7 Are you taller than your friend?

★ Yes, I am.
★ No, I'm not.
★ We're the same.

b) *1.32* Listen again. What are Nyree's answers?
1   No, she isn't.

Grammar spot
Comparative adjectives

Nyree is **taller than** Tamsin.
Tamsin is **more talkative than** me.
Are you **better at sport than** your friend?

Grammar spot
Object pronouns

She's friendlier than **me**.
I'm more hard-working than **her**.
Ben is taller than **him**.

She's the same age as **us**.
He's more talkative than **you**.
Nyree is funnier than **them**.

 Grammar page 99

❸ Speaking

a) Complete the survey about you and a friend. Don't show your classmates.

b) Work with a classmate. Ask and answer.

Are you older than your friend?

No, I'm not.

❹ Listening and speaking

a) 1.33 Listen. Look at the picture. Who are the sentences about – Pete or Ben?

Pete, 11

Ben, 12

b) 1.33 Listen again and write your answers – Ben or Pete.

1 Ben

c) Now make sentences about Ben and Pete with:

Pete/Ben … is … than Ben/Pete.
Pete's/Ben's … is … than Ben's/Pete's ….

more comfortable   younger   better   bigger
smaller   longer   older   more hard-working

Ben's chair is more comfortable than Pete's chair.

Pete is younger than Ben.

My English file

Compare yourself with a friend or someone in your family. Write six sentences with *I'm … than him/her. He's/She's … than me.*

<u>My brother and I</u>

He's older than me.

He's taller than me.

Spelling tip

bi**g** – bi**gg**er
fun**ny** – funn**ier**

❺ Check your English

a) Write a list of comparative adjectives from these words.

talkative   tall   good   friendly
hard-working   funny   old   young
comfortable   long   short   big   small

talkative	*more talkative*
tall	*taller*
good	*better*

b) Write three questions from these words:

1 than | shorter | is | your classmate's hair
your hair | ?

2 you | than | more talkative | your classmate
are | ?

3 than | your bag | bigger | is
your classmate's bag | ?

c) Then answer the questions with *Yes, it is. No, it isn't. Yes, I am.* or *No, I'm not.*

10 Wayne's world: My family

1 Presentation

a) *1.34* Listen and read. Find the people and things Wayne talks about in the picture.

Sally's my grandmother and today's her 70th birthday. What's special about Gran? Well, she's the oldest person in my family and she's holding the youngest person, Gina. Gina's my baby cousin and she's only nine months old. I also think Gina's the most beautiful person in my family!

That's Uncle Tony behind the sofa. Look at the present he's giving Gran. It's so big! Tony's the most generous person in our family. He always gives us great presents.

And that's my sister, Tina. Tina's the fittest person in my family and she's also the best at sport. She's crazy about exercise and loves going to the gym.

And that's my mum, Linda. She's the friendliest person in my family and she's also the most talkative. She loves parties and chatting to people.

And me. Well, umm. I'm the most handsome person in my family!

b) *1.34* Listen again. Complete the chart about Wayne's family.

Name	Relationship	Special thing
Sally	*grandmother*	*oldest*
Gina		
Tony		
Tina		
Linda		

Real English

Gran   chatting   crazy about

Grammar spot
Superlative adjectives

She's the **oldest** person in my family.
Tony is the **most generous** person in my family.
She's the **best** at sport.

❷ Grammar practice

Look at the picture in Activity 1. Make sentences with:

Sally's the oldest person in Wayne's family.

> most talkative   most generous   fittest
> most beautiful   most handsome
> oldest   friendliest   youngest

Sally   _____
Gina   _____
Tony   's the   _____   person in Wayne's family.
Tina   _____
Linda   _____
Wayne   _____

❸ Speaking

a) Write three questions to ask your teacher with *Who is the … person in your family*? Use the words in the box in Activity 2.

Who is the oldest person in your family?

b) Ask your teacher your questions.

> Who is the oldest person in your family?

> My grandfather. He's 87 years old.

❹ Pronunciation

 Listen and repeat.

talkative
hard-working
comfortable
beautiful
generous
funniest
friendliest
messiest

❺ Writing

a) Work with a classmate. Look at the picture. Complete the sentences with *Pete, Ben, Meg* or *Pete's, Ben's, Meg's*.

1 Ben

1 _____ is the oldest.
2 _____ is the youngest.
3 _____ is the best at Maths.
4 _____ hair is the longest.
5 _____ hair is the shortest.
6 _____ bag is the biggest.
7 _____ desk is the messiest.

b) 〔1.36〕 Listen and check.

❻ Song ♪♫♪

〔1.37〕 Find the song *Our family* on page 91.

❼ Check your English

Complete the questions with the superlative. Then answer the questions.

1 tallest

1 Who is the _____ student in your class? (tall)
2 Who is _____ student in your class? (hard-working)
3 Who is _____ at sport in your class? (good)
4 Who is the _____ student in your class? (friendly)
5 Who is the _____ student in your class? (talkative)
6 Who has got the _____ hair in your class? (long)

11 Which is faster?

1 Presentation

a) (1.38) Listen and read. Think about your answers.

Animal quiz

Can you guess the answers to these questions?

Fast

1 Which is faster:

 or

a snail   a tortoise?

2 Which is the fastest animal:

a cheetah   a deer   a horse?

Intelligent

1 Which is more intelligent:

 or

a dog   a mouse?

2 Which is the most intelligent animal:

an owl   a chimpanzee   a dolphin?

DANGEROUS

1 Which is more dangerous:

 or

a cobra   a scorpion?

2 Which is the most dangerous insect:

an ant   a fly   a mosquito?

Strong

1 Which is stronger:

 or

a horse   a camel?

2 Which is the strongest animal:

a bear   a buffalo   an elephant?

b) Work with a classmate. Write your answers.

1   *A tortoise is faster than a snail.*

c) (1.39) Listen and check.

Grammar spot
Comparative/superlative adjectives

Comparative
A tortoise is **faster than** a snail.
A cobra is **more dangerous than** a scorpion.

Superlative
A cheetah is **the fastest** animal.
A mosquito is **the most dangerous** insect.

(00) Grammar page 98

❷ Grammar practice

Look at the animals in Activity 1. Complete with the comparative or superlative of the adjective in brackets.

1   faster

1   A tortoise is ____ than a snail. (fast)
2   A cheetah is the ____ land animal. (fast)
3   A cobra is ____ than a scorpion. (dangerous)
4   A mosquito is the ____ insect. (dangerous)
5   A dog is ____ than a mouse. (intelligent)
6   A chimpanzee is ____ animal. (intelligent)
7   A camel is ____ than a horse. (strong)
8   An elephant is the ____ animal. (strong)

❸ Speaking

a) Listen to Annie and her classmate Billy. Billy is a terrible bragger.

Tom's really nice.

Oh, I'm nicer than him. In fact, I'm the nicest boy in the school.

And Mary's really intelligent.

Oh, I'm more intelligent than her. In fact, I'm the most intelligent student in the school.

b) Now work with a classmate. Continue the dialogue. Use four of these or four of your own ideas.

> nice   intelligent   generous   strong   friendly
> polite   hard-working   good at sport   funny
> handsome   kind   fit   beautiful   friendly

Annie: Tom's really polite.
Billy: Oh, I'm more polite than him. In fact, I'm the most polite boy in the school.
Annie: And Mary's really...

Study tip

Write a list of comparative and superlative adjectives.

Adjective	Comparative	Superlative
big	bigger	biggest
good	better	best
bad	worse	worst

My English file

a) Write a quiz. Write about animals, people and things. Use Activity 1 to help you.

1   Which are more expensive: cars or bicycles?

2   Which do you think is the best football team: Manchester United, Barcelona or Juventus?

b) Then exchange quizzes with a classmate.

c) Answer your classmate's quiz.

❹ Check your English

a) Choose the correct word.

1   Are you the *taller*/*tallest* student in your class?
2   Are you *taller*/*tallest* than your friend?
3   Is your friend *better*/*best* at Maths than you?
4   Who is the *better*/*best* at Maths in your class?
5   Are mice *more intelligent*/*most intelligent* than dogs?
6   What is the *more intelligent*/*most intelligent* animal in the world?

b) Then answer the questions.

1   No, I'm not. John's the tallest student in my class.

12 City or country?

❶ Reading

a) *1.41* Listen and read. Steve lives in Bristol, a city in England. Does he want to live in the country?

There are some good things about living in a village in the country. It's quieter than the city. Also, it's more beautiful and it's cleaner because there aren't many cars and buses.

However, there are a lot of bad things about living in the country. It's more boring than living in the city. Cinemas, cafés and swimming pools are a long way from your home. Also, it's more difficult to go shopping in the country because there aren't many shops. But the worst thing about living in the country is that it's more difficult to find friends there. It's easier to find friends in a city because there are more kids the same age as you.

I live in Bristol and I like living in the city because it's more exciting and more interesting than living in the country.

b) Read again. What are three good things about living in the country? What are three bad things? Write notes.

Good things: quieter, more ...
Bad things: more boring, ...

❷ Listening

a) *1.42* Listen. Helen lives in Charfield, a village 20 miles from Bristol. Does she think that it is better to live in the city?

b) *1.42* Listen again. What does Helen say? Choose the correct words.

1 There are *lots of/ some* good things about living in a city.
2 Cities are *boring/exciting*.
3 Most kids *have got/haven't got* the money to go to cinemas or cafés.
4 It's *easier/more difficult* to meet friends in a city.
5 Friends live *close/a long way* from my house.

❸ Speaking

a) (*1.43*) **Listen to the questions. Think about your answers.**

1 Which is quieter: a city or the country?
2 Which is more beautiful?
3 Which is cleaner?
4 Where are there more cars and buses?
5 Which is more exciting?
6 Where are there more things to do?
7 Where is shopping more difficult?
8 Where is it easier to find friends?
9 Where is it easier to hang out and play with friends?

b) **Work with a classmate. Take it in turns to ask the questions.**

> Which is quieter: a city or the country?

> The country.

❹ Writing

Write about where you live. What are the good things and what are the bad things?

> The Country
>
> There are some good things and some bad things about living in the country. I think a good thing is that there are lots of trees …
> I think a bad thing is …

Writing tip
Connecting words

It is quieter than the city. **Also**, it is more beautiful …

However, there are lots of bad things about living in the country. …

Fun spot

Associations

a) Match the adjectives in the word cloud to the pictures.

1 – fun, fast

comfortable

fit long *dark* old

short hard-working

young talkative big

generous beautiful

tall *messy* friendly

intelligent

polite good small funny

fun strong interesting fast

dangerous expensive

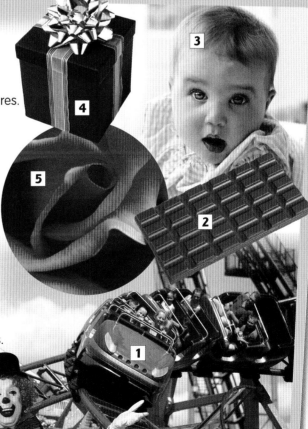

b) Then compare your answers with your classmates.

Review

Check you can do these things.

1 I can compare myself with my friend.

Think of a friend and make sentences. Use the adjective in brackets.

My friend's name is Simon. He's older than me. I'm better at sport than him. ...

My friend's name is ...		
I'm He's/She's	____ (old) ____ (good at sport) ____ (talkative) ____ (funny) ____ (hard-working) ____ (friendly) ____ (tall)	than him/her. than me.

2 I can ask questions using comparative adjectives.

Write four questions.

1 chair | is | comfortable | your | more?

2 bigger | than | my bag | your bag | is | ?

3 you | than | taller | me | are | ?

4 me | younger | than | you | are | ?

3 I can use these object pronouns.

What is this boy saying? Make sentences with *He's taller than...* and these pronouns:

me   you   him   her   us   them

1. He's taller than us.

2.

3.

4.

5.

6.

4 I can remember people in Wayne's family and use superlative adjectives.

a) Complete the sentences. Use the initial letters to help you.

1 Sally's the o____ person in Wayne's family.

4 Tony's the m____ g____ person in Wayne's family.

2 Gina's the y____ and the m____ b____ person in Wayne's family

5 Tina's the f____ person in Wayne's family and she's also the b____ at sport.

3 Linda's the f____ person in Wayne's family and she's also the m____ t____.

b) Now match the sentences in a) with this information.

a She's crazy about exercise.

b He always gives us great presents.

c Today's her 80th birthday.

d She loves parties and chatting to people.

e She's only nine months old.

5 I know when to use the comparative and the superlative.

Complete the dialogue with:

> old   older   oldest   good   better   best

A: Who's the ____ boy in your class?
B: Tony.
A: How ____ is he?
B: He's nearly twelve.
A: Is he ____ than Susan?
B: No, he isn't. Susan's 12.
A: And who's the ____ at sport in your class?
B: Gisella. She's in the school netball team.
A: Is she ____ than you?
B: Yes, she is. I'm not very ____ at sport.

6 I know how to write superlative and comparative adjectives.

Copy and complete this table.

Adjective	Comparative	Superlative
big	*bigger*	*biggest*
good		
intelligent		
funny		
dangerous		
fit		
friendly		
bad		

Extra special

 Word games

1 Opposites

What is the opposite of these words? Use the initial letters to help you.

1 t____/short

5 straight/c____

2 big/s____

6 old/n____

3 young/o____

7 l____/short

4 d____/light

2 Picture puzzles

a) Match the words with the pictures.

> **1** dinner **2** the table **3** rubbish **4** a bicycle **5** your teeth **6** the dog **7** the carpet

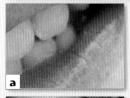
a

b

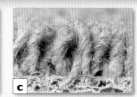
c

d

e

f

g

b) Then write phrases with these words:

vacuum   ride   lay   cook   clean   recycle   feed

vacuum the carpet

3 Odd word out

What is the odd word out?

1 packet bottle plastic can jar

2 morning night week afternoon evening

3 swimming surfing sailing hanging out skating

4 chimpanzee lorry tortoise snail cheetah

5 metal paper cardboard glass box

4 Word jigsaw

a) Match the beginnings and the ends of the words.

1 *intelli*   a) *some*

2 *comfor*   b) *working*

3 *gen*   c) *ative*

4 *beaut*   d) *gent*

5 *danger*   e) *table*

6 *hard-*   f) *erous*

7 *hand*   g) *iful*

8 *talk*   h) *ous*

b) Then think of a person or thing to match the words in a).

intelligent – Albert Einstein

Mini project

1 Read Marina's descriptions of Beyoncé and Rihanna. Do you agree with her?

Beyoncé is a R&B singer.

She is also a songwriter, film star and fashion designer.
She is American. She is older than Rihanna. Two of her most successful songs are "Crazy in Love" and "Baby Boy". Two of her films are The Pink Panther and Dreamgirls.

Rihanna is a singer.

She is from Barbados in the West Indies. She is taller than Beyoncé. Her most famous song is called "Umbrella". I think Rihanna is a better singer than Beyoncé. I think she is more beautiful than Beyoncé.

Marina

2 Write a profile comparing two famous people.

3 Show your descriptions to your classmates. Answer any questions.

Module 4
Rules

13 We have to wear a school uniform

❶ Picture search

1.44 Find these in the pictures:

| jackets | ties | trousers | shirts |
| skirts | slippers | school bag |

❷ Presentation

a) *1.45* Listen to Masami. Do you have to do the same things in your school?

My school in Japan

Masami, 12

1 We have to wear a uniform at our school. Our uniform's dark blue and grey. We wear jackets, ties, and white shirts. Boys wear trousers and girls wear skirts.

We have to be at school at 8:30. Our lessons start at 8:40. **2**

3 When we get to school we have to change our shoes. We always wear slippers inside the school.

4 At the beginning of a lesson, we have to stand up and greet our teacher with a bow. We have to put our hand up to ask questions. Then we have to stand up when we answer our teacher's questions.

5 Our school bags are really heavy. That's because we have to study ten school subjects!

6 At the end of the day we have to clean and tidy our classroom.

b) *1.45* Listen again. Now vote. What's the most difficult thing Masami and his classmates have to do?

❸ Comprehension

Answer these questions.

1 At what time do the students have to be at school?
2 What are the students doing in picture 3?
3 What do they have to do at the beginning of a lesson?
4 Why are their school bags really heavy?
5 When do the students clean and tidy their classroom?

Grammar spot
Have to (obligation)

Do we **have to wear** a school uniform?
Yes, we **do**./No, we **don't**.

We **have to wear**
We **don't have to wear** a school uniform.

👀 Grammar page 100

❹ Writing and speaking

a) *1.46* Look at the pictures in Activity 2 and listen to the questions. Think about your answers.

b) Then ask and answer with: *Do you have to ...? Yes we do./No, we don't.*

> Do you have to wear a school uniform?

> No, we don't.

c) Work with two or three classmates. Write lists about things you have to and don't have to do at your school.

We have to...
1 switch off our mobile phones.
2 ...

We don't have to...
1 clean and tidy our classroom.
2 ...

Grammar spot
Have to (obligation)

Does he/she **have to get** ready for school?
Yes, he/she **does**./No, he/she **doesn't**.

He/She **has to get**
He/She **doesn't have to get** ready for school.

👀 Grammar page 100

❺ Listening

a) *1.47* Listen to Ian. Why does he like Sundays?

b) *1.47* Listen again. What does Ian have to do on Sunday? Make sentences with: *He has to* or *He doesn't have to.*

1 He doesn't have to get up early.

1 get up early
2 do some chores
3 wear a school uniform
4 get ready for school
5 do homework
6 go to bed early

❻ Check your English

a) Write two questions with these words. Then answer the questions.

1 have to | does | do any chores | your | friend | ?

2 a | tie | you | have to | do | wear | ?

b) Write true sentences about the things you have to and don't have to do today.

I have to buy a notebook.
I don't have to do any homework.

14 Rules of sport

❶ Vocabulary

a) *1.48* Listen. Match the verbs with the pictures.

1 catch **2** kick **3** carry **4** head **5** throw **6** hit **7** roll **8** hold

a b c d e f g h

b) *1.49* Listen and check.

❷ Presentation.

a) *1.50* Listen and read. Think about your answers.

Rules of sport!

Answer these questions.

1 Basketball

  a) Can you carry the ball?

  b) Do you have to throw the ball?

  c) Can you catch the ball?

2 Bowling

  a) Can you throw the ball?

  b) Do you have to roll the ball?

  c) Can you stand on the line?

3 Tennis

  a) Do you have to hit the ball with a racket?

  b) Do you have to wear a sweatband?

  c) Can you head the ball over the net?

4 Football

  a) Can only the goalkeeper catch the ball?

  b) Do the two teams have to wear different colours?

  c) Can you carry the ball?

b) *1.50* Work with three or four classmates. Listen again. Then answer with:
Yes, you can./No, you can't./Yes, you do./No, you don't.

Basketball – a) No, you can't.

c) *1.51* Listen and check your answers.

Grammar spot
Can (permission)

Can we **carry** the ball?
Yes, you **can**./No, you **can't**.

You **can carry** the ball.
You **can't carry** the ball.

Grammar page 100

 **Remember!**

Full and short form!
cannot = can't

❸ Grammar practice

a) Work with a classmate. Write three questions about a popular sport with *Can you... ?* Use your dictionaries to help with new vocabulary.

Football
Can you throw the ball?
Can you hit the ball with your hand?
Can you roll the ball?

b) Take it in turns to ask your classmates your questions.

In football, can you throw the ball?

Yes, you can.

c) Make sentences with *You can...* or *You can't...*

In bowling, you can't throw the ball.

1 Bowling

4 Football

2 Tennis

5 Bowling

3 Basketball

6 Tennis

❹ Writing and speaking

a) Look at the places. Think about these questions.

1 What things can you do there?
2 What things can't you do?
3 What things do you have to do?

swimming pool   park

classroom

b) Write some ideas.

You can write in your notebooks.
You can't eat or drink.
You have to pay attention.

c) Then read your ideas to your classmates. Can they guess the place?

You can't eat or drink.

Is it a classroom?

Yes, it is.

My English file

Write some rules about a sport or a game you know with *can, can't, have to.*

Ice hockey

Your team can only have six players on the ice.
You can't kick the puck.
You have to wear a helmet and gloves.

❺ Song ♪♫♪

(1.52) Find the *Dream Park* on page 91.

❻ Check your English

Make true sentences about basketball. Choose the correct words.

1 You *can/can't* kick the ball.
2 You *can/can't* catch the ball.
3 You *have to/don't have to* throw the ball.

15 Wayne's world:
This is what we eat in a week

❶ Picture search

1.53 Listen. Match the words with the food and drink in the picture.

biscuits – g

| biscuits apples chicken salad meat cheese cola tomatoes sugar |
| bread potatoes eggs fish pasta milk oranges bananas salt |

❷ Presentation

a) *1.54* Look at the picture and listen.

b) *1.54* Listen again. What do Wayne and his family eat and drink? Make true sentences.

They eat a lot of salad. They don't eat many biscuits. They don't drink much cola.

They eat/drink	a lot of …
	a lot of …
They don't eat/drink	many …
	much …

Grammar spot
Much/many/a lot of

Uncountable
How **much** salad do you eat?
I eat **a lot of** salad./I don't eat **much** salad.

Countable
How **many** biscuits do you eat?
I eat **a lot of** biscuits./I don't eat **many** biscuits.

👓 Grammar page 101

❸ Grammar practice

a) Work with a classmate. Put these words in two lists.

biscuit salt meat cheese sweet tomato
bread pasta sugar potato milk egg chip

countable   *uncountable*
biscuit   salt
...   ...

b) *1.55* Listen and check.

Study tip

Countable and uncountable nouns

Can you count eggs?

Yes, I can. One egg, two eggs, three...

Can you count salt?

No, I can't!

❹ Speaking

a) Work with a classmate. Look at the picture in Activity 2. Ask and answer questions with:

How much/many … do you eat drink/drink?
I eat/drink a lot of …
I don't eat/drink much/many …
I don't eat/drink …

How much cola do you drink?

I don't drink cola.

How many apples do you eat?

I eat a lot of apples.

b) Make notes of your classmates' answers.
cola – X, apples – a lot of

c) Then tell the rest of your class about your classmate.

❺ Pronunciation

1.56 Listen and practise the Waiter Rap.

Bread, biscuits and bananas,
Cola, pasta and sweets.
Spinach, ice-cream and sandwiches,
With lots and lots of oranges.
Meat, carrots and tomatoes,
Eggs, salad and potatoes.
Chicken, chocolate and cheese,
Fish and rice, yes, please!

❻ Check your English

a) Make true sentences about you. Choose the correct words.

1 I *eat a lot of/don't eat much/many* spinach.
2 I *eat a lot of/don't eat much/many* eggs.
3 I *drink a lot of/don't drink much/many* water.
4 I *eat a lot of/don't eat much/many* meat.
5 I *eat a lot of/don't eat much/many* chips.

b) Complete the questions with *How much* or *How many*. Then answer about you.

1 _____ milk do you drink?

2 _____ sweets do you eat?

3 _____ pasta do you eat?

4 _____ apples do you eat?

16 Rules, rules, rules

❶ Reading

a) Read and match the rules with the pictures.

Beach volleyball is a very popular game all over the world but especially on the beaches of Brazil, America and Australia. These are the rules.

1 You play beach volleyball with bare feet. You can't wear shoes or trainers.

2 You serve the ball by throwing the ball into the air with one hand and hitting it with your other hand. The ball has to go over the net.

3 You have to hit the ball back over the net with your hand or arm. The ball can't touch the ground.

4 You can pass the ball three times to your team-mates. Then you have to hit it back over the net.

5 You can't touch the net with your hands and arms.

b) Read again. Find these words in the text. Do you know or can you guess what they mean?

1 bare feet **2** serve **3** hit back **4** pass **5** touch

❷ Listening

a) (1.57) Ian goes to school in Shetland and has a very strict French teacher. Listen. Do you have the same rules in your English classes?

b) (1.57) Listen again. What are the missing verbs?

1 We can't _____ with our friends in her lessons.
2 We have to _____ to our classmates.
3 We have to _____ new words in our notebooks.
4 We have to _____ our French textbooks to every lesson.
5 We don't have to _____ French all the time.
6 We can _____ questions in English.
7 We have to _____ 70% in tests.

❸ Speaking

a) *1.58* Listen to the questions. Think about your answers.

Weekends

1 Can you stay in bed all morning?
2 Do you have to tidy your room?
3 Can you hang out with your friends?
4 Do you have to do homework?
5 Can you watch a lot of TV?
6 Do you have to go to bed early?
7 Do you have to go for a walk?

b) Then work with a classmate. Take it in turns to ask and answer the questions.

> Can you stay in bed all morning?

> Yes, I can.

b) Tell the rest of the class about your classmate.

> Susana can stay in bed all morning.

❹ Writing

Work with a classmate. Choose one of these subjects to write about. Use *can*, *can't*, *have to*, *don't have to*.

1 Sport
Write a list of rules for a sport or game you know. Write the name of the sport, but don't show your classmate. Use Activity 1 to help you. Then read your rules to your classmate. Can he/she guess the name of the sport?

2 School
Write a list of rules for your school and classroom. Use Activity 2 to help you. Then exchange lists with your classmate. Are your rules the same as your classmate's?

3 Home
Write a list of home rules. Use Activity 3 to help you. Then exchange lists with your classmate. Are your rules the same as your classmate's?

Fun spot

a) *1.59* Listen. Fiona is very fussy. Can you guess why she likes some food and doesn't like other food?

b) *1.60* Listen and check.

Review

Check you can do these things.

1 I can talk about things I have and don't have to do.

a) Make true sentences about yourself. Choose the correct words and complete the sentences. Use the initial letters to help you.

> I have to do chores.

1   I *have to/don't have to* d____ chores.
2   I *have to/don't have to* g____ u____ early at the weekend.
3   I *have to/don't have to* b____ on time for lessons.
4   I *have to/don't have to* g____ ready for school on Sunday.
5   I *have to/don't have to* e____ food I don't like.

2 I know these eight sports verbs.

Mime these actions.

1   catching a ball

2   kicking a ball

3   throwing a ball

4   heading a ball

5   carrying a ball

6   hitting a ball

7   rolling a ball

8   holding a ball

3 I can ask questions with *Can you* ...? and *Do you have to* ...?

a) Complete these four questions with *Can you...*? or *Do you have to* ...?

1   ____ wear slippers in the classroom?
2   ____ hang out with your friends any time you like?
3   ____ eat food you don't like?
4   ____ sit with your friends in class?

b) Then answer the questions about you.

4 I know how to use *How many* and *How much.*

Look at the picture. Then take it in turns to close your books and ask and answer the questions.

Ask with *How much/How many ... do you eat/drink?*

Answer with *I eat/drink a lot of .../I don't eat/drink much / many ...*

How much cheese do you eat?

I eat a lot of cheese.

5 I can understand rules.

Read this list of swimming pool rules. Match the rules with the pictures.

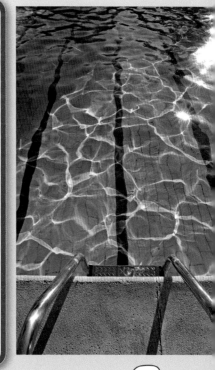

1	You can't jump into the water.	a) 
2	You have to use the steps.	b)
3	You have to shower.	c) 
4	You can't throw balls.	d) 
5	You can't wear shoes.	e) 

Extra special

Sports quiz

How much do you know about sport? Work with three or four classmates. Write your answers.

1 How many players are there in a volleyball team?

A Eleven

B Six

C Ten

2 Match the pictures and the sports.

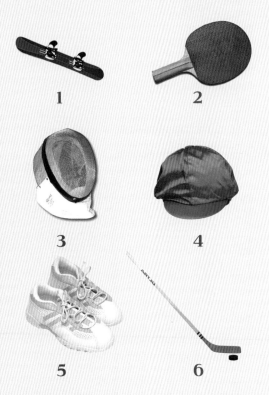

1

2

3

4

5

6

a) athletics
b) fencing
c) snow boarding

d) ice hockey
e) horse riding
f) table tennis

3 How long is the marathon race?

A 30 kilometres

B 28 kilometres

C 42 kilometres

4 Where were the first Modern Olympic Games?

A Athens

B London

C Barcelona

5 How often are the Olympic Games?

A Every year

B Every four years

C Every ten years

6 Which is the odd sport out and why?

swimming golf rugby baseball tennis

7 Match the ball to the sport.

a) golf   *d) table tennis*
b) tennis   *e) baseball*
c) American football

8 What athletics' event is this?

A *The high jump*
B *The pole vault*
C *The long jump*

9 How long is a football match?

A *45 minutes*
B *90 minutes*
C *180 minutes*

Mini project

a) Read Karen's quiz. Write answers to the questions.

How much do you know about music?

1 **What is the name of this musical instrument?**
   A guitar
   B keyboards
   C harp

2 **Match the dance with a country.**

   1 Samba   a) Austria
   2 Tango   b) Spain
   3 Waltz   c) Brazil
   4 Flamenco   d) Argentina

3 **What are the names of three famous composers?**

4 **What is the odd word out?**
   hip-hop piano jazz country pop classical

   Karen

b) Write a quiz about one of your favourite topics. Here are some ideas.
   Art   Animals   TV shows
   Films   Books   Celebrities

c) Ask your classmates to write answers to your quiz.

17 Famous people

❶ Vocabulary

2.01 Listen. Match the words with the pictures.

> artist   dancer   inventor   writer   scientist

a  b  c  d  e

❷ Presentation

a) *2.02* Listen and read. Find out about these famous people.

Fact file: Famous people

1 Who was Anna Pavlova? She was a dancer. She was Russian. She was born in 1881. She is one of the greatest dancers of all time.

2 Who was Leonardo da Vinci? He was an artist, an inventor and a scientist. He was Italian. He was born in 1452. His most popular painting is the Mona Lisa.

3 Who were Marie and Pierre Curie? They were scientists. Marie Curie was Polish. Pierre Curie was French. She was born in Poland in 1867. He was born in France in 1859. They are famous for the discovery of radium.

4 Who were the Brontë sisters? They were writers. They were English. Their names were Anne, Charlotte, and Emily. Charlotte Brontë's most popular book is *Jane Eyre*.

b) Read again. Then complete the table.

Name	Occupation	Nationality
Anna Pavlova	*dancer*	...
Leonardo da Vinci		
Marie Curie		
Pierre Curie		
The Brontë sisters		

Grammar spot
Past tense of verb *be*

Who **was** Anna Pavlova?   She **was** a dancer.
Was she Russian?   Yes, she **was**.

Who **were** Marie and Pierre Curie?
They **were** scientists.
Were they Russian?   No, they **weren't**.

 Grammar page 102

❸ Grammar practice

Ask and answer about:

1 Anna Pavlova
2 Leonardo da Vinci
3 Marie and Pierre Curie
4 The Brontë sisters

> Who was Anna Pavlova? She was a dancer.

❹ Vocabulary

a) *2.03* Listen and repeat. Then match the word with the famous people in the pictures.

> singer   teacher   athlete
> astronomer   queen

1 Cleopatra, Egyptian, 69 BC–30 BC

2 Jesse Owens, American, 1913–1980

3 Maria Montessori, Italian, 1870-1952

4 Luciano Pavarotti, Italian, 1935–2007

5 Nicolaus Copernicus, Polish, 1473–1543

b) *2.04* Listen and check.

Study tip
How to say and write dates.

1913 (Nineteen thirteen)   1506 (Fifteen, oh six)

2009 (two thousand and nine)

❺ Listening

a) *2.05* Look at the people in the pictures and listen. Why are they famous?

1

2

b) *2.05* Listen again. Then choose the correct words.

1 He was an *artist/a singer/a musician*.
He was *French/Spanish/German*.
His name was Pablo Picasso

2 They were *musicians/film stars/artists*.
They were *American/English/Polish*.
Their names were Chico, Harpo and Groucho Marx.

❻ Speaking

a) Think of a famous person or famous people. Write the name/names, occupation and nationality. Don't show your classmates

> Marx Brothers, Film stars, American

b) Take it in turns to ask and answer.
Use: *Was he/she …? / Were they …?*

> Were they scientists?   No, they weren't.

My English file
Find out about a famous person and write some sentences about him or her.

Fryderyk Chopin

He was a composer. He was Polish and he was born in 1810. He was most famous for …

❼ Check your English

Complete the dialogue with *was, wasn't, were, weren't*.

A: Who _____ Pierre and Marie Curie?
B: They _____ scientists.
A: _____ they American?
B: No. He _____ French. She _____ Polish.
A: _____ she born in France?
B: No, she _____. She _____ born in Poland.

18 Nineteen hundred

❶ Presentation

a) (2.06) Look at the pictures and listen. Can you guess what three activities people didn't do in 1900?

1 Did people play football in 1900?
   Yes, they did./No, they didn't.

2 Did they use computers?
   Yes, they did./No, they didn't.

3 Did they travel in space?
   Yes, they did./No, they didn't.

4 Did people ski in the mountains?
   Yes, they did./No, they didn't.

5 Did they cycle to work?
   Yes, they did./No, they didn't.

6 Did they watch TV?
   Yes, they did./No, they didn't.

b) (2.07) Listen and check. Then ask and answer the questions.

Did they play football in 1900?

Yes, they did.

Grammar spot
Past simple questions

Did people **play** football?

Yes, they **did**.

No, they **didn't**.

❷ Writing and speaking

a) What was life like when your teacher was your age? Write three questions to ask your teacher.

Did people have mobile phones?
Did people play computer games?
Did people wear trainers?

b) Ask your questions.

Did people have mobile phones?

No, they didn't.

Grammar spot
Past simple (regular verbs)

They play**ed** football.   They **didn't play** football.
They watch**ed** TV.   They **didn't watch** TV.

 Grammar page 102

❸ Grammar practice

a) Choose the correct word to make true sentences about people in 1900.

1   People *played*/*didn't* play football.
2   They *used*/*didn't use* computers.
3   They *travelled*/*didn't travel* in space.
4   They *skied*/*didn't ski* in the mountains.
5   They *cycled*/*didn't cycle* to work.
6   They *watched*/*didn't watch* TV.

b) *2.08* Listen and check.

❹ Pronunciation

2.09 Listen and repeat.

played   used   listened   travelled
skied   cycled   phoned   watched

Spelling tip

use – us**ed**   cycl**e** – cycl**ed**
phon**e** – phon**ed**   travel – trave**lled**

❺ Speaking

a) Look at the questionnaire and read. Think about your answers.

Last weekend

How many of these activities did you do last weekend?

1 Did you phone your friends?

2 Did you listen to music?

3 Did you watch TV?

4 Did you use a computer?

5 Did you travel by bus?

6 Did you play with your friends?

b) Work with a classmate. Take in turns to ask and answer the questions.

Did you phone your friends?   No, I didn't.

c) Report back to the class about your classmate.

Michelle didn't phone her friends. She listened to music....

❻ Check your English

a) Write three questions to ask your classmates about last weekend.

1   *Did you go to the cinema?*
2   *...*
Then ask and answer questions.

Did you go to the cinema?   No, I didn't.

b) Make sentences about last weekend. Use these verbs and a dictionary to help you with new vocabulary.

| **1** played | **2** used | **3** listened | **4** travelled |
| **5** skied | **6** cycled | **7** phoned | **8** watched |

1   *I played computer games.*
2   *I used a microwave.*

19 Every word is true

❶ Presentation

a) *2.10* Look at the pictures and listen. Use the pictures to help you understand. Is Professor Moriarty telling Sherlock Holmes the truth?

> This is what I did yesterday, Holmes. I'm telling the truth.

In the morning I took a taxi to Hyde Park. I sat on the grass in the park and read a magazine. I left the park at a quarter to 12 and went to Piccadilly Circus by underground. I had lunch in an Italian restaurant. In the afternoon I bought some new shoes. In the evening I saw a play. I got back to my hotel at half past 10.

Professor Moriarty

b) *2.10* Listen again. Make notes of all the differences between Moriarty's statement and the pictures.

1   by bus not by taxi

> No, Moriarty. Your statement isn't true. It's full of lies.

Grammar spot
Past simple (irregular verbs)

I **took** a taxi to Hyde Park.
I **sat** on the grass and **read** a magazine.

❷ Grammar practice

a) What did Professor Moriarty do yesterday? Write true statements. Use these words:

took	sat	read	left	had
went	saw	bought	got	

a bus	a newspaper	on a bench
by taxi	at a quarter past twelve	
at twelve o'clock	a film	
a Chinese restaurant	a new shirt	

In the morning he took a bus to Hyde Park. He ...

b) (2.11) Then listen and check.

❸ Speaking

a) (2.12) Listen to Sherlock Holmes and Professor Moriarty.

Holmes: Did you take a taxi to Hyde Park?
Moriarty: Yes, I did.
Holmes: No, you didn't take a taxi. You took a bus.
Holmes: And did you sit …

b) Then work with a classmate. Play Holmes and Moriarty. Ask and answer with:

Did you take a taxi to Hyde Park?

Yes, I did.

No, you didn't …

❹ Writing and speaking

a) How many of these things did you do last weekend? Write a list. Don't show your classmates.

I watched TV. I read a magazine. ...

I had a shower.
I played computer games.
I sat in the park.
I watched TV.
I read a magazine. I bought sweets.
I listened to music.
I got up late.
I took a bus.
I cycled to a friend's house.
I went swimming.
I phoned a friend.
I saw a film.

b) Work with two or three classmates. Ask questions with *Did you … ?* Answer with *Yes, I did. No, I didn't.*

Did you buy sweets?

No, I didn't.

❺ Song ♪♫♪

(2.13) Find *Last summer* on page 92.

❻ Check your English

a) Complete with *go* and *went*.

A: Did you _____ swimming last weekend?
B: No, I didn't _____ swimming. I _____ to the cinema.

b) Now work with your classmates. Make other mini-dialogues with:

have/had   buy/bought   read/read
watch/watched   listen/listened

A: Did you have pizza?
B: No, I didn't have pizza. I had a sandwich.

20 School trip

❶ Reading

a) *2.14* Read Calum's diary. Where was his trip to? How many places did he visit?

My school trip

Calum (12), Leicester, England

06:00	I got up early and went to school.
07:00	I sat next to Mick on the coach and we had sandwiches for breakfast. The traffic was really bad and it took 3 hours to get to London.
10:00–13:30	The first thing we did was go to the Natural History Museum. We saw a lot of interesting things but the thing I liked most was the dinosaur – it was enormous!
13:30–14:30	We got back on the coach and went to the Tower of London. On the way we had more sandwiches for lunch!
14:30–16:00	The Tower of London was fantastic. We saw the Beefeaters and the Crown Jewels.
16:00–17:30	Then we walked to the London Eye. It was a long walk and we weren't very happy. I was hungry and had another sandwich.
18:00–18:40	The London Eye was brilliant. At the top we were 135m above London. The views were amazing and we saw Big Ben.
19:00–22:00	We stopped on the way back home and had fish and chips in a restaurant. It was really nice to have fish and chips after all those sandwiches!

b) Find these words in the diary. Can you guess what they mean?

1 coach **2** traffic **3** enormous
4 on the way **5** the top **6** view

c) Match the pictures with places in Calum's diary.

a   Crown Jewels

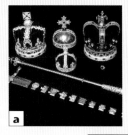
a

b

c

d

e

❷ Speaking

a) *2.15* Look at Calum's diary and listen.

1 What time did he get up?
2 Who did he sit next to on the coach?
3 Where did he go first?
4 What did he like best there?
5 Where did he go next?
6 What did he see there?
7 What did he see at the top of the London Eye?

b) Then work with a classmate. Ask and answer.

What time did he get up?   At six.

❸ Listening

a) *2.16* Listen to Anne talking about her school trip. What did she see first?

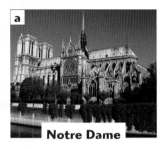

a

Notre Dame

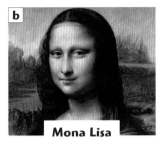

b

Mona Lisa

c

Eiffel Tower

d

River Seine

b) *2.16* Listen again. Can you guess the meaning of these words?

1 paintings   **2** boat trip
3 steps   **4** lift   **5** view

❹ Writing

Write a diary of a school trip. Use Calum's diary as a model. Use your dictionaries to help you with new vocabulary.

> My school trip to Disneyland
> monday 8:30 We went to Disneyland Paris by coach. It took 14 hours! On the way we sang songs.
> Tuesday 8:00 We arrived in Disneyland and the first thing we did was have breakfast. We had...

Writing tip
Useful expressions

The first thing we did was go to the Science Museum.
It took 3 hours to get to London.
The thing I liked most was the dinosaur.
On the way we had more sandwiches.

It was **fantastic/brilliant/amazing**.

Fun spot

Alibi game

a) Write an alibi about what you did yesterday.

> Yesterday I left home at ten o'clock. I had cereal for breakfast. Then I took a taxi to the park...

Yesterday I left home at *(time)*. I had *(name of food)* for breakfast. Then I took *(a bus/a taxi)* to the park. I met my friend *(name of friend)* and we played *(name of sport)*. Then we had lunch in *(name of restaurant)*. In the afternoon we went shopping. I bought *(a/some ...)*. In the evening we went to the cinema and saw *(name of film)*. The film began at *(time)* and finished at *(time)*. I got home at *(time)*. Then I watched *(name of TV programme)* on TV.

b) Exchange statements with a classmate. Tell your classmate what you did yesterday. Try not to make any mistakes.

> Yesterday I left home at...

Review

Check you can do these things.

1 I can use the past tense of *be* and occupations.

a) Complete with *was* or *were* and the occupation. Use the initial letters to help you.

1 Anna Pavlova was a dancer.

1 Anna Pavlova _____ a _____.

2 The Brontë sisters _____ w_____.

3 Cleopatra _____ a _____.

4 Leonardo da Vinci _____ an a_____.

5 Marie and Pierre Curie _____ s_____.

6 Jesse Owens _____ an a_____.

7 Nicolaus Copernicus _____ an a_____.

b) Now complete the dialogue with *was* or *were*.
A: Who _____ the Marx Brothers? _____ they singers?
B: No, they _____n't. They _____ film stars.
A: And who _____ Pablo Picasso? _____ he a musician?
B: No, he _____n't. He _____ an artist.

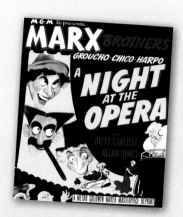

2 I know these six nationalities.

Match the nationality with the famous people in Activity 1. Write your answers.

1 The Brontë sisters.

1 English **2** Russian **3** Italian **4** Polish **5** American **6** French **7** Egyptian

3 I can ask and answer past questions with *Did*.

Look at the picture. Ask and answer questions about life in 1900 with *Did people … in 1900*? Use these words.

> travel in space   use computers   watch TV   cycle to work   play football   ski in the mountains

Did people travel in space?   No, they didn't.

4 I know these regular and irregular past tense verbs.

a) Find five regular and eight irregular past tense verbs in this wordsearch. Write a list.

Played, ...

o	w	t	x	j	p	o	n	b	v	n
a	e	g	o	t	a	l	t	o	a	n
u	n	b	e	v	g	i	n	u	y	x
s	t	t	k	e	d	s	k	g	j	i
w	b	c	o	z	d	t	o	h	e	f
a	j	p	h	o	n	e	d	t	h	w
t	n	l	t	e	k	n	o	u	y	v
c	e	a	r	g	r	e	a	d	n	m
h	c	y	c	l	e	d	m	x	e	s
e	a	e	n	g	l	y	n	m	r	i
d	n	d	e	q	y	s	a	t	h	u

b) What did Ian do last Saturday? Use the initial letters to help you.

1   In the morning he got up early and had a shower.

1   In the morning he _____ up early and _____ a s_____ .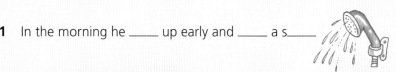

2   He _____ t_____ and he_____ to m_____ .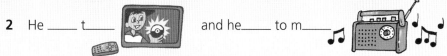

3   Then he _____ a b_____ into town and _____ some new j_____ .

4   In the afternoon he _____ to the p_____ and _____ f_____ .

5   Then he _____ on the g_____ and _____ a m_____ .

6   In the evening he p_____ his f_____ and they w_____ to the c_____ .

7   They _____ a comedy f_____ .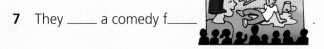

5 I can use the past simple to ask and answer questions.

Choose the correct word.

A: Did you *go/went* to the park yesterday?
B: Yes, we *do/did*. We *go/went* in the afternoon.
A: Did you *play/played* handball?
B: No, we *don't/didn't* *play/played* handball. We *play/played* tennis.

Extra special

Mini-play

a) Look at the picture. What's Olivia holding?

b) 2.17 Listen. Can you think of a good title for this mini-play?

Daisy: What is it?

Olivia: This is the great, the fantastic, the amazing Swipple.

Colin: Swipple?

Olivia: Yes. And I've got only five of them.

Frank: Only five?

Olivia: Yes, only five.

Daisy: How much are they? Are they expensive?

Olivia: No, they're not expensive; they're cheap. These are the best, the smallest, the fastest Swipples in the world!

Frank: Wow. That's amazing!

Olivia: Yes, it is! Do you have to do chores at home?

Frank: Yes, I have to clean my room.

Olivia: Right. Then the Swipple is for you.

Frank: Brilliant!

Olivia: And do you like playing computer games?

Colin: Yes, I do.

Olivia: Then the Swipple is for you, too.

Colin: Great!

Daisy: Is the Swipple for me too?

Olivia: When's your birthday?

Daisy: It's on 21st April.

Olivia: Yes, you're lucky. It's for you too.

Daisy: Wonderful!

Colin: What are Swipples made of?

Olivia: They're made of metal, plastic, glass and…er… sugar.

Colin: Sugar?

Olivia: Yes, the sweetest sugar in the world.

Colin: Fantastic!

Olivia: So boys and girls. Who wants a Swipple?

Children: Me, me, me!

Bob:	What's happening?
Daisy:	Olivia's selling Swipples.
Frank:	Yes, but we bought them all. I bought one.
Daisy:	And I bought one too.
Colin:	And I bought three!
Bob:	Can I see them?
Frank:	Sure. They're the smallest Swipples in the world.
Daisy:	And the best.
Colin:	And the fastest.
Bob:	Umm. But what do they do?
Children:	What do they do?
Bob:	Yes, what do they do?
Daisy:	Er, well… we don't know what they do.
Frank:	Yes, that's right. What do they do? Hey, Olivia!
Colin:	Yes. Where is she?
Children:	Olivia, Olivia, Oliva…

c) **2.17** Listen again. Then read the play with your classmates.

Memory challenge

Learn your lines by heart.

Mini project

a) Read Paul's story. What do you think is the most fantastic part of his story?

My fantastic day

I got up late and had a dinosaur for breakfast.

Then I went to the park and played a game of football with David Beckham.

Then I went shopping and bought a Ferrari.

In the afternoon I flew to New York.

In the evening I drove around New York City in a limousine.

And then I woke up!

Paul

b) Make a poster about a fantastic day. Use pictures from magazines to help you write the story.

c) Show your poster to your classmates.

21 Wayne's world:
A bad start to the day

❶ Presentation

a) *2.18* Listen and read. Use the picture to help you understand.

09:50

Zoë:	Are you ok, Wayne?
Wayne:	No, not really.
Zoë:	Why? What's the matter?
Wayne:	Oh, I had a really bad start to the day. I woke up late.
Zoë:	Were you late for school?
Wayne:	No, I arrived on time, but I forgot my Science homework.
Zoë:	Oh, dear.
Wayne:	Yes and I didn't close my bedroom window or switch off the lights.

08:07

b) *2.18* Listen again. Then read with your classmate.

Real English

Are you ok?
Oh, dear.

❷ Comprehension

a) Look at the picture. Choose the correct words.

1 He *put on*/*didn't put on* his school uniform.
2 He *made*/*didn't make* his bed.
3 He *fed*/*didn't feed* his fish.
4 He *drank*/*didn't drink* his orange juice.
5 He *ate*/*didn't eat* his cereal.

6 He *switched off*/*didn't switch off* the TV.
7 He *forgot*/*didn't forget* his sandwiches.
8 He *closed*/*didn't close* his door.
9 He *cleaned*/*didn't clean* his teeth.
10 He *picked up*/*didn't pick up* his clothes.

b) *2.19* Listen and check.

❸ Grammar practice

Past simple – regular and irregular verbs

a) Copy and complete this list.

Regular		Irregular	
switch off	*switched off*	wake up	*woke up*
clean	____	forget	____
close	____	put on	____
open	____	make	____
pick up	____	feed	____
arrive	____	drink	____
		eat	____

b) *2.20* Now listen and repeat.

👀 Grammar page 105

❹ Listening and speaking

a) *2.21* Listen. How many of these things did you do this morning?

1	wake up	6	eat
2	put on	7	switch off
3	make	8	forget
4	feed	9	clean
5	drink	10	pick up

b) Work with your classmates. Ask and answer:

Did you wake up late?

Yes, I did. or No, I didn't.

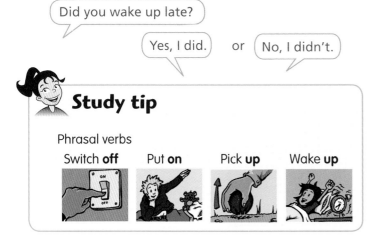

Study tip

Phrasal verbs

Switch **off**   Put **on**   Pick **up**   Wake **up**

❺ Memory game

Play the Memory Game with your classmates. Mime the actions.

I woke up this morning and got dressed.

I woke up this morning and got dressed. Then I combed my hair.

I woke up this morning, got dressed and combed my hair. Then I cleaned my …

❻ Check your English

Write six true sentences about what you did and didn't do this morning. Use these verbs:

wake up   switch off   clean   close   pick up
forget   put on   make   open   feed   drink   eat

I didn't wake up late. I didn't make my bed. I fed my dog. I forgot my pen. I ate some cereal. I didn't pick up my clothes.

Remember!

Infinitive

Question: Did you **wake** up?

Past tense

Affirmative: I **woke** up.

Infinitive

Negative: I didn't **wake** up.

Lesson
Objective | • Talking about what
you did in the past

22 A day out at the seaside

❶ Picture search

2.22 Find these things in the picture.

| postcards sandcastle donkeys shade beach fishermen wetsuit café sea |

❷ Presentation

a) *2.23* Listen. Find the Glooms in the picture.

b) *2.23* Listen again. What are the missing words?

| sat rode spoke swam built wrote wore threw hung out ran |

Last summer the Glooms had a day out at the seaside. Martha _____ in the sea and Sam and Pam _____ a huge sandcastle. Cynthia _____ in the shade and Mandy _____ a lot of postcards. Rudolph _____ in a café and Helga _____ to two fishermen. Gordon _____ a donkey and Vincent _____ along the beach. Vera _____ a wetsuit and Bernard _____ balls for Bonehead.

c) *2.23* Listen and check.

❸ Speaking

Look at the picture in Activity 2. What did the Glooms do at the seaside? Ask and answer with *What did ... do? He/She ...*

What did Vincent do?

He ran along the beach.

Grammar spot
Past time expressions

I went shopping **last weekend**.
Did you go out **yesterday**?

Grammar spot
Past simple – *Wh-* questions

When did the Glooms travel to the seaside?
What did Cynthia read?

❹ Listening and speaking

a) 2.24 Rudolph Gloom is talking to a friend about last Saturday. Listen and finish the questions.

1   I got up late.
    What time did you get up?

1   I got up late.
    What time …?
2   I phoned a friend.
    Who …?
3   We then met in town.
    Where …?
4   We had a snack.
    What …?
5   We went to the park.
    How …?
6   We saw some classmates.
    Who …?
7   We talked.
    What …?

b) 2.24 Listen again. Then repeat the conversation with a classmate.

c) Now make yor own conversation with your classmate.

I played computer games.

What game did you play?

I played ...

My English file

Write sentences with these past time expressions:

> yesterday   last night   last weekend
> last summer   last Saturday afternoon

I saw a film yesterday. I played a computer game last night.
I...

❺ Check your English

a) Write three questions with these words. Then answer the questions about you.

1   *What time did you get up this morning?*
    I got up at 7:30.

1   this morning   did   what time
    you   get up   ?

2   hang out with   did   last weekend
    who   you   ?

3   you   go   where   last summer   did   ?

b) Make sentences about what you did in the past. Use these verbs.

> sat   rode   spoke   swam   built
> wrote   wore   threw   hung out   ran

I sat next to my friend. I rode a horse.

23 Gulliver in Lilliput

1 Presentation

a) 2.25 Listen and read. Use the pictures to help you understand.

My name is Lemuel Gulliver and I'm a ship's doctor. On 5th November, 1699 there was a terrible storm. There were huge waves and my ship hit a rock. Then I swam to an island.

The next morning I woke up on the beach. There was a very small man a few centimetres from my nose. He was a soldier and had a bow and arrow and he was afraid.

There were hundreds of soldiers and they all had bows and arrows. I tried to stand up but the soldiers shot arrows at me. The arrows were very small but I didn't try to stand up again.

I was very hungry. I asked for food but the soldiers didn't understand. They didn't speak English. I pointed to my mouth and they understood. Then, the soldiers fed me.

I was very tired after my meal and slept. That night the soldiers took me to their city. A thousand horses pulled the wagon.

b) 2.26 Read again. Then find these in the pictures.

| storm waves ship rock bow |
| soldier arrow horses wagon |

Study tip

Telling a story – Time expressions

On 5th November, 1699 there was …
The next morning I woke up …
Then I swam …
That night the soldiers took…

❷ Comprehension

a) (2.27) Listen to the questions. Work with a classmate and make notes of your answers.

1   a rock

1   What did Gulliver's boat hit?
2   Where did he swim?
3   Where was Gulliver when he woke up the next morning?
4   What did Gulliver try to do?
5   What did the soldiers shoot at Gulliver?
6   What did he ask for?
7   Where did they take Gulliver that night?

b) Take it in turns to ask and answer.

> What did Gulliver's boat hit?   A rock.

Grammar spot
There was/were

There was a terrible storm.
There were huge waves.

🔖 Grammar page 104

❸ Listening

a) (2.28) Gulliver saw this street in Lilliput. Listen to the questions.

b) (2.28) Listen again and answer the questions with:

> Yes, there was/there were.   or

> No, there wasn't/there weren't.

c) Now make true sentences about the picture using the words in the box.

There were some people. There wasn't a shop.

people	shop	benches	horses	cinema
soldiers	children	church	palace	bicycles
trees	theatre	houses	dogs	cats	café

❹ Pronunciation

a) (2.29) Listen and repeat.

bring	brought	run	ran
build	built	say	said
drink	drank	sit	sat
eat	ate	speak	spoke
feed	fed	swim	swam
forget	forgot	take	took
hang	hung	throw	threw
make	made	understand	understood
meet	met	wake	woke
read	read	wear	wore
ride	rode	write	wrote

b) (2.30) Listen. Can you hear the infinitive or the past tense? Say the answer.

> Bring   Infinitive

c) Now test your classmate. Read the infinitive or past tense.

❺ Song ♫

(2.31) Find *Gulliver's story* on page 92.

❻ Check your English

Think of somewhere you went. For example, a party, the cinema. Write some sentences about it with *There was/wasn't …*, *There were/weren't …*

> My sister's birthday party
> There were a lot of people.
> There was a lot of food.
> There was good music…

24 My life

❶ Reading

a) (2.32) Listen and read Anka's biography. Where did Anka live? Where does she live now?

My biography

1997	I was born on 26th February in Poland.
1998	I took *my first steps* and said my first words. My first word was kot (cat in English).
1999	I got my first pet, a dog.
2000	My brother Kuba was born on 7th May.
2001	I went to nursery school. I had *an operation* in hospital
2002	I got my first bike for my birthday. I learnt how to ride my bike.
2003	I started primary school and met my friends Magda and Sonia. I learnt how to swim.
2004	I began *guitar lessons* and I went skiing for the first time.
2005	We went on holiday to the Baltic coast and I saw the sea for the first time.
2006	I went on my first skiing holiday with my class. I *won a music competition*.
2007	My family moved to Peterborough in England. I made a new friend. Dana is from the Czech Republic and I had my first conversation in English with her.
2008	I started secondary school. I wore a school uniform for the first time and made my first English friends. My grandmother visited us in the summer and we went to a *theme park* called Alton Towers. At Christmas we went back to Poland for two weeks and I was very excited and happy because I saw my friends Magda and Sonia again.

b) Read again. Match these pictures with the phrases in the text.

1  **2**  **3**  **4** 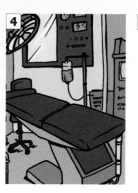 **5**

c) When did Anka do these things?

1   1998

1 take first steps
2 say first word
3 ride a bike
4 go to primary school
5 learn to swim
6 play the guitar
7 go on first skiing holiday
8 see the sea
9 win a music competition
10 speak English
11 wear a school uniform

❷ Speaking

a) (2.33) Listen to the questions. Look at Activity 1 and think about your answers.

1 When was Anka born?
2 What was her first word?
3 When did she learn how to ride a bike?
4 Who did she meet in 2003?
5 Where did her family move to in 2007?
6 Who did she meet there?
7 What did she wear for the first time in 2008?
8 Who visited Anka's family in England?
9 Where did Anka and her family go at Christmas?

b) (2.33) Listen again. Then work with your classmates. Take it in turns to ask and answer.

> When was Anka born?　　In 1997.

❸ Listening

a) (2.34) Listen. Where does Owen live now? Where did he live?

b) (2.34) Listen again. Find the missing information.

1 Owen was born in _____.
2 Owen's family moved to Kenya when he was _____ years old.
3 They lived there for _____ years.
4 Owen went to _____ and _____ school in Kenya.
5 He spoke _____ and Swahili in Kenya.
6 His family moved back to Cardiff in _____.
7 He liked life in _____ more than life in _____.

❹ Writing

Write your biography. Use Anka's biography as a model.

> My biography
> 1998 I was born in St Gallen, Switzerland.
> 1999 I took my first steps and said my first word.
> 2000 …

Fun spot

Memory game

a) Work with two or three classmates. Look at the picture. Try to remember everything. You have two minutes.

b) (2.35) Close your book. Then listen to the questions and write your answers.

1 *Yes, there were.*
2 *No, there wasn't.*

c) (2.36) Open your book and c1heck your answers.

Review

1 I know these eighteen irregular past tense verbs.

a) Read out the verbs.

> woke up, forgot, ...

wokeupforgotputonmadefeddrankateswamsatrodespokebuiltwroteworethrewhungoutranwent

b) Make sentences about Wayne's bad start to the day.

1   Wayne woke up late.

1 Wayne w____ up l____

2 He f____ his S____ h____

3 He p____ on his s____ u____

4 He didn't s____ off the l____

5 He didn't c____ the w____

6 He didn't m____ his b____

7 He f____his f____

8 He a____ his c____

9 He d____ his o____ j____

10 He c____ his t____

11 He didn't p____ up his c____

c) Make sentences about the Glooms with the words in A and B.

A	B
1 Martha swam	**a)** a wetsuit.
2 Sam and Pam built	**b)** a donkey.
3 Cynthia sat	**c)** in a café.
4 Mandy wrote	**d)** along the beach.
5 Rudolph hung out	**e)** in the sea.
6 Helga spoke	**f)** a lot of postcards.
7 Gordon rode	**g)** a huge sandcastle.
8 Vincent ran	**h)** in the shade.
9 Vera wore	**i)** balls for Bonehead.
10 Bernard threw	**j)** to two fishermen.

2 I can answer these past simple questions.

Answer these questions. Write full sentences.

1   I went to bed at half past eleven.

1   What time did you go to bed last night?
2   Where did you go last weekend?
3   How did you travel to school this morning?

4   What did you have for breakfast?
5   When did you do your homework?
6   What time did you get up this morning?

3 I know the story of Gulliver arriving in Lilliput.

Work with a classmate. How quickly can you complete the story with these words?

> small   waves   morning   arrows   took   thirsty   meal   English   bow   horses   island
> food   soldiers   stand up   wagon   water   centimetres   hit   storm   hungry   mouth

1)   storm

My name is Lemuel Gulliver and I'm a ship's doctor. On November 5th, 1699 there was a terrible ¹____ . There were huge ²____ and my ship ³____ a rock. I swam to an ⁴____ .

The next ⁵____ I woke up on the beach. There was a very ⁶____ man a few ⁷____ from my nose. He was a soldier and had a ⁸____ and arrow.

There were hundreds of ⁹____ and they all had bows and arrows. I tried to ¹⁰____ but the soldiers shot arrows at me. The ¹¹____ were very small but I didn't try to stand up again.

I was very ¹²____ and ¹³____ . I asked for ¹⁴____ and ¹⁵____ but the soldiers didn't understand. They didn't speak ¹⁶____ . I pointed to my ¹⁷____ and they understood. The soldiers fed me.

I was very tired after my ¹⁸____ and slept. That night the soldiers ¹⁹____ me to their city. A thousand ²⁰____ pulled the ²¹____ .

4 I can use *there was* and *there were*.

Make correct sentences about the street Gulliver saw in Lilliput. Choose the correct words.

1   There *was/were* some houses.
2   There *was/were* a theatre.
3   There *wasn't/weren't* any shops.
4   There *wasn't/weren't* a church.

Extra special

Gulliver in Lilliput

a) (2.37) Listen and read the rest of the story.

1

I woke up inside an old temple. It was one of the biggest buildings in Lilliput. That day I met the Emperor. He spoke to me but I didn't understand him.

2

The Emperor sent six of his best teachers and I learnt their language. I learnt the country's name was Lilliput and the people were called Lilliputians.

3

The Lilliputians called me Man-Mountain and they were still afraid of me. The Emperor's soldiers looked in my pockets. They found my comb, my watch, my diary and my pistol. They took away my things.

4

The Lilliputians were now my friends. I visited the city and played with the children in the streets.

5

One day the emperor asked for my help. A country called Blefuscu planned to attack Lilliput.

We eat our eggs like this.

They eat their eggs like this.

6

The Emperor explained why the Lilliputians and Blefuscudians were enemies.

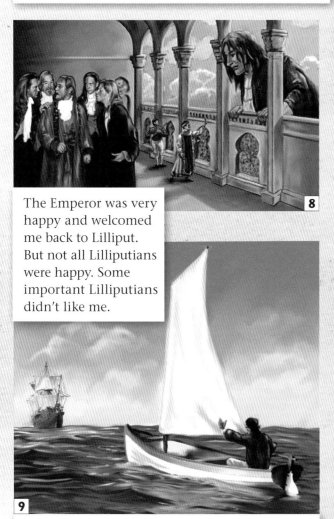

7

I didn't want Blefuscu to attack Lilliput. I swam to Blefuscu and took all their ships back to Lilliput.

8

The Emperor was very happy and welcomed me back to Lilliput. But not all Lilliputians were happy. Some important Lilliputians didn't like me.

9

I left Lilliput and went to Blefuscu. The Emperor of Blefuscu was kind to me but I wanted to go home. I left Blefuscu on a boat. An English ship found me and took me home.

b) Read again. Look up new words in a dictionary.

Mini project

a) Read about Paul's hero. Do you know his name?

My hero

My hero was born in South Africa in 1918.

He studied law and became a politician.

He fought for Human Rights.

He spent 27 years in prison.

He became famous all over the world.

He was the President of South Africa from 1994 to 1999.

Paul

b) Write about a famous person. Don't write the name.

c) Read about your classmates' heroes. Can you guess the names?

Looking at the future

25 Holiday plans

❶ Presentation

a) *2.38* Listen and read. Match the pictures with the questions.

1 – h

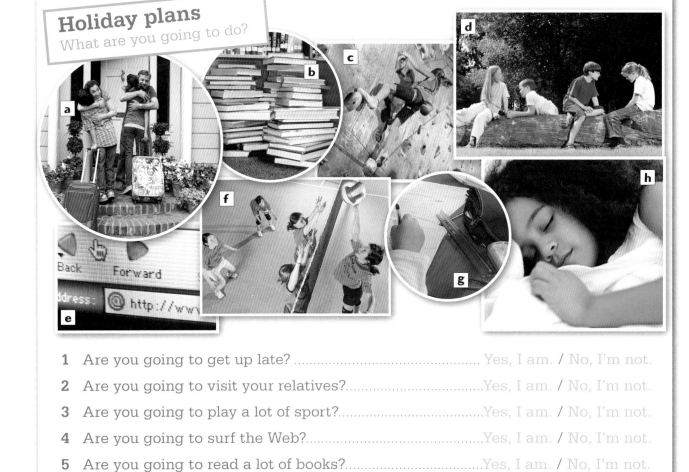

Holiday plans
What are you going to do?

Back   Forward

ddress: @ http://ww

1 Are you going to get up late? .... Yes, I am. / No, I'm not.

2 Are you going to visit your relatives? .... Yes, I am. / No, I'm not.

3 Are you going to play a lot of sport? .... Yes, I am. / No, I'm not.

4 Are you going to surf the Web? .... Yes, I am. / No, I'm not.

5 Are you going to read a lot of books? .... Yes, I am. / No, I'm not.

6 Are you going to learn something new? .... Yes, I am. / No, I'm not.

7 Are you going to hang out with your friends? .... Yes, I am. / No, I'm not.

8 Are you going to do any school work? .... Yes, I am. / No, I'm not.

b) *2.38* Listen again. Write answers with *Yes, I am* or *No, I'm not*. Don't show your classmates.

❷ Class survey

a) Work with a classmate. Ask and answer the questions.

Are you going to get up late?

Yes, I am.   or   No, I'm not.

b) What are your classmates going to do in the holidays? Write the results on the board.

For example

Holiday Plans
Get up late – 7 students
Visit relatives ...

Grammar spot
Going to (plans and intentions)

Are you **going to** get up late?   Yes, I am./No, I'm not.
I'm **going to**/I'm **not going to** get up late.

(Grammar page 104)

❸ Grammar practice

Look at the survey. Make sentences with
I'm going to …/I'm not going to …

1   I'm going to get up late. or
   I'm not going to get up late.

1 … get up late.
2 … visit my relatives.
3 … play a lot of sport.
4 … surf the Web.
5 … read a lot of books.
6 … learn something new.
7 … hang out with my friends.
8 … do school work.

❹ Writing and speaking

a) Write a list of three things you are going to
do next holidays. Look up any new vocabulary
in a dictionary.

Help parents
Visit grandparents
Paint room

b) Work with a classmate. Tell them what you
are going to do.

I'm going to help my parents in our shop.
I'm going to visit my grandparents.
I'm going to paint my room.

c) Now ask and answer. Find out what your
classmate is going to do next holidays.

Are you going to help your parents?

Yes, I am.   or   No, I'm not.

❺ Speaking and listening

a) Nyree is going to stay at Tamsin's house
tonight for a sleepover. Look at the picture
and find these things.

sweets   DVD   cola   camera
computer game   mobile phone

b) What are Nyree and Tamsin going to do
tonight? Make sentences with *They are going
to…* and these words:

They are going to watch a film.

watch	eat	drink	listen	play	phone	take
sweets	cola	their friends	a computer game			
a film	some photos	to music				

c) (2.39) Listen and check.

❻ Check your English

a) Make questions with these words. Then
answer the questions about you.

1 tonight watch are TV you going to ?

2 you on Saturday meet going to are
your friends?

3 do are this evening your homework
going to you ?

b) Make true sentences with:

1 I'm going to … this summer.
2 I'm not going to … tomorrow.

26 Wayne's world:
Trip to New York City

❶ Presentation

a) *2.40* Listen and read. Find the places Wayne talks about on the map.

New York City

I'm really excited because this summer my family's going to spend five days in New York City. We're going to stay with my aunt and uncle. They live in the Bronx but we're going to spend most of our time in Manhattan. My uncle is a taxi driver and he's going to drive us around Manhattan. He's going to show us the **Empire State Building**. We're also going to take a cruise around **New York Harbour** and visit the **Statue of Liberty**. I'm going to watch baseball at the **New Yankee Stadium** with my uncle and my mum is going to buy clothes on **Fifth Avenue** with my aunt. Tina's going to run in **Central Park**. And on the last night we're all going to see a musical on **Broadway**.

b) *2.40* Listen and read again. Then look at the map and match the pictures to the places.

a – Broadway, b – ....

c) *2.41* Listen and check.

❷ Comprehension

a) *2.42* Look at the map again and listen to the questions about Wayne's trip to New York City. Write notes.

1 – 5 days

b) *2.42* Close your books. Listen again. Answer the questions.

How much time are Wayne's family going to spend in New York?

Five days.

Grammar spot
Going to (plans and intentions)

I'm
He/She's **going to spend** five days in New York City.
We/They're

(Grammar page 104)

❸ Grammar Practice

What is Wayne's family going to do this summer?

They're going to spend five days in New York.

		spend five days	the Statue of Liberty
They're		take a cruise	in Central Park
Wayne's uncle's		visit	on Broadway
Wayne's	going to	watch baseball	around New York Harbour
Wayne's mum		buy clothes	in New York City
Tina's		run	on Fifth Avenue
		see a musical	at the New Yankee Stadium

❹ Writing

a) Look at the questionnaire. Plan a trip with a classmate by answering the questions.

> #### Our trip
>
> 1 Where are you going to visit?
>
>
>
> the seaside   the mountains   a lake
>
> 2 How much time are you going to spend there?
>
> three days   a week   two weeks
>
> 3 How are you going to travel there?
>
>
>
> by train   by coach   by plane
>
> 4 Where are you going to stay?
>
>
>
> in a hotel   in a hostel   on a campsite
>
> 5 What are you going to do?
>
> We're going to …
>
> *We're going to the mountains. We're going for two weeks. …*

b) Read your description to your classmates. Are any of their descriptions the same as yours?

❺ Game

Play the long sentence game. Say what you are going to do in the holidays.

I'm going to ride my bike.

I'm going to ride my bike and play tennis

I'm going to ride my bike, and play tennis and get up late.

I'm going to …

❻ Check your English

What are their plans for this weekend? Complete the sentences with *going to*.

1 (I'm …)

2 (We're …)

3 He's …

4 She's …

81

27 Let's go rafting

❶ Picture search

2.43 Listen. Match these attractions with the pictures on the Funland map.

horse riding   rafting   roller coaster   Haunted Castle   picnic   go-karting

❷ Presentation

a) 2.44 Listen and read. What do Amy, Dan and Jim want to do at Funland?

Dan: Great! Let's go rafting.
Amy: Yes, I want to go rafting.

Dan: How about you, Jim? Do you want to go rafting?
Jim: No, I don't want to go rafting. It's too cold.

Dan: I know. Let's ride the roller coaster.
Jim: Yes, that's a good idea.
Dan: How about you, Amy? Do you want to ride the roller coaster?
Amy: No, I don't. It's too scary.

Amy: I know. Let's go horse riding.
Dan: No, I don't want to go horse riding. I don't like horses.

Jim: I know. Let's have a picnic.
Amy/Dan: Yes, That's a great idea. Let's do that.

Real English

How about you?
It's too cold/too scary.
I know.
That's a great idea.

b) 2.44 Listen again. Then read the dialogue with two classmates.

❸ Comprehension

Look at the pictures again. Then answer the questions.

1 Who wants to go rafting?
2 Who doesn't want to ride the roller coaster?
3 Who doesn't want to go horse riding?
4 Who wants to have a picnic?

Grammar spot
Want to/Let's + infinitive

Want to
Do you **want to go** rafting? Yes, I do./No, I don't.
I **want to go** rafting.
I don't **want to go** rafting.

Let's
Let's **ride** the roller coaster.

❹ Grammar practice

a) What do you want to do at Funland? Make suggestions with *Let's* or *Do you want to* …

1 Let's go rafting./Do you want to go rafting?

1 go rafting
2 ride the roller coaster
3 go horse riding
4 have a picnic
5 go go-karting
6 visit the Haunted Castle

b) Listen to your classmates' suggestions. Then answer with: *Yes, good idea. Let's do that.* Or *No, I don't want to do that. It's too…*

Let's go rafting.

Yes, good idea. Let's do that. | or | No, I don't want to do that. It's too…

❺ Listening

a) 2.45 Listen to Amy, Jim and Dan talking after their picnic.

b) 2.45 Listen again and answer these questions.

1 What do Amy and Dan want to do?
2 Why doesn't Jim want to do that?
3 What does Jim want to do?
4 Do Amy and Dan want to do that too?

❻ Pronunciation

a) 2.46 Listen and practise the tongue twister.

Ronald rode a scary red roller coaster after riding horses with Rosie.

b) 2.47 Now say the tongue twister really fast.

My English file
Plan a great day out with a friend. Use:
A: Let's …
B: No, I don't want to …
It's too cold/scary/difficult/boring/…
A: What do you want to do?
B: I want to …
A: That's a good idea! Yes, let's …

A: Let's go to the park.
B: No, I don't want to ….

❼ Song

2.48 Find *Let's go to Funland* on page 93.

❽ Check your English

a) Choose the correct words.

1 Let's *go/to go* to the cinema.
2 Do you want *watch/to watch* TV.
3 Let's *play/to play* tennis.
4 I don't want *have/to have* breakfast.

b) Match the beginning and endings of the words.

A	B
1 haunted	nic
2 raft	castle
3 roller	riding
4 pic	coaster
5 horse	karting
6 go-	ing

28 Loch Ness holiday

❶ Reading

a) (2.49) Read the text. Where is Nessie House?

Nessie House is on the famous Loch Ness in Scotland and it's the perfect place for an exciting holiday. You can stay in rooms for four, eight or twelve people. During the day you can learn three new activities with expert teachers and instructors. And in the evening you can go to the Monster Café and play table tennis, video games, board games or watch films in our cinema room.

Nessie House Activity Centre

Where we are:

Nessie House

Loch Ness

b) Imagine you are going to Nessie House with three classmates. Complete the booking form.

Booking form

1 How are you going to travel to Nessie House?

By train ☐

By coach ☐

By car ☐

2 Which room do you want to book?

Room for 4 people ☐

Room for 8 people ☐

Room for 12 people ☐

3 What activities do you want to do during the day? Tick three boxes.

Canoeing ☐   Acting ☐

Rock climbing ☐   Arts and Crafts ☐

Water skiing ☐   Horse riding ☐

4 Which is your favourite evening activity? Tick one box.

Table tennis ☐   Video games ☐

Board games ☐   Films ☐

5 What meals do you want to have at Nessie House?

Breakfast ☐   Lunch ☐   Dinner ☐

You can also order packed lunches.
Tick this box to order packed lunches. ☐

❷ Speaking

a) *2.50* Look at the booking form. Listen and practise asking the questions.

1 How are you going to travel to Nessie House?
2 Which room do you want to book?
3 What activities do you want to do during the day?
4 Which is your favourite evening activity?
5 What meals do you want to have at Nessie House?
6 Do you want a packed lunch?

b) Work with a classmate. Ask and answer the questions.

> How are you going to travel to Nessie House?

> By car.

❸ Listening

a) *2.51* Look at the booking form and listen to Joanna.

b) *2.51* Listen again. Are these sentences true or false?

1 Twenty students went on the school trip to Scotland.
2 They travelled to Loch Ness by plane and coach.
3 Joanna chose canoeing, rock climbing and acting for her activities.
4 They had three meals a day in Nessie House.
5 They saw the Loch Ness Monster.

❹ Writing

Write a description of your perfect holiday centre. Use the description in Activity 1 as a model.

> Lake House Holiday Centre
> Lake House is on the shore of Lake Como in Italy. It's a perfect place for an exciting water sports holiday. You can ...

Fun spot

Picnic game

a) *2.52* Listen. Mr Smith is going to take his class for a picnic in the country.

b) Why can Ann go on the picnic, but Jane and David can't go? Play the Picnic game with your teacher to find out. Take it in turns to make sentences with *I'm going to take*

c) *2.53* Listen to the secret.

Review

Check you can do these things.

1 I can use *going to* to talk about plans and intentions.

Complete the sentences with a verb and then choose the correct words. Make true sentences about your plans for this summer.

1 I'm *going to/not going to* _____ out with my friends.

2 I'm *going to/not going to* _____ my relatives.

3 I'm *going to/not going to* _____ in bed all morning.

4 I'm *going to/not going to* _____ school work.

5 I'm *going to/not going to* _____ a lot of sport.

2 I can remember what Wayne and his family are going to do in New York City.

Complete with these verbs:

| see | run | spend | drive | take | stay | watch | visit | show | buy | live |

I'm really excited because this summer my family's going to ^{1}_____ five days in New York City. We're going to ^{2}_____ with my aunt and uncle. They ^{3}_____ in the Bronx but we're going to ^{4}_____ most of our time in Manhattan. My uncle is a taxi driver and he's going to ^{5}_____ us around Manhattan. He's going to ^{6}_____ us the Empire State Building. We're also going to ^{7}_____ a cruise around New York Harbour and ^{8}_____ the Statue of Liberty. I'm going to ^{9}_____ baseball at the New Yankee Stadium with my uncle and my mum is going to ^{10}_____ clothes on Fifth Avenue with my aunt. Tina's going to ^{11}_____ in Central Park. And on the last night we're all going to ^{12}_____ a musical on Broadway.

3 I know the names of these six activities.

Write the activities. Use the initial letters to help you.

1    2    3   4   5   6

h____ r____   r____   g___ k____   r___ c____   c____   w___ s____

4 I can make suggestion with *Let's*.

What are the people saying? Make sentences with *Let's*.

1    2    3

Let's ...   Let's ...   Let's ...

5 I can ask what people want to do.

Make questions with these words. Then work with a classmate and ask and answer the questions.

1   the roller coaster | you | ride | do | want to | ?

2   you | want to | a picnic | have | do | ?

3   play | video games | do | you | want to | ?

6 I can write about what I want to do.

Write three sentences about what you want to do this weekend.

For example
I want to go to the cinema.

7 I can make sentences with *don't want to*.

Complete the sentences.

1   I don't want to …   It's too scary.
2   I don't want to …   It's too difficult.
3   I don't want to …   It's too boring.
4   I don't want to …   It's too cold.

> I don't want to go rock climbing. It's too scary.

Extra special

Hot Spot end of book quiz!

1 Play this game in teams.
2 Write your answers to the questions.
3 You can't remember? Don't worry. You can look in your book!
4 The first team with 15 correct answers is the winner!

1 Who can see this from his window?

2 What is the name of this country?

3 What chores are Mandy, Rudolph and Sam and Pam doing?

4 What are these four things made of?

5 What are the names of the six foods in an English breakfast?

6 Who is more hardworking – Nyree or her friend Tamsin?

7 How old are these two people and what are their names?

8 Steve thinks there are some good things about living in the country but can you remember three bad things?

9 Can you remember three things that Masami has to do at school?

10 What two things can you do in basketball and what two things can't you do?

11 Why doesn't Fiona like some food?

12 What is the name of this building and can you remember one thing you can see there?

13 What did the soldiers find in Gulliver's pockets?

14 What are the names of these two places in New York?

15 Can you remember three things you can do at Funland?

Mini project

a) Read Terry's advertisement. Do you think Newtown Linford is a good place for a holiday?

Holiday advertisement

Welcome to Newtown Linford

I live in a village called Newtown Linford. It's in Leicestershire, England and it's a lovely place for a holiday.

How to get there:

By car – The M1 motorway
By air – East Midlands Airport
By train – Leicester Station and then by bus

A good place to stay

The Bradgate B&B. It costs £30 per person per night.

A good place to visit

Bradgate Park. You can see deer and an old castle. This castle was the home of Lady Jane Grey.

A good place to eat

Chanwood Teashop has tea and cakes. The cakes are delicious.

Terry

b) Make a holiday advertisement for your hometown.

c) Show your advertisement to your classmates.

Songs

All about me

My name's Gemma
I live in Richmond Street
I've got long brown hair
and very big feet

I love sport and music
I can roller-skate, I can swim
I can play the piano
and the violin

Chorus
  What about you
  What can you do?
  Do you like football
  or going to the zoo?
  When's your birthday?
  How old are you?
  Do you like purple
  green, grey or blue?

I don't like reading
but I'm good at P.E.
I love playing tennis
I hate watching TV

I've got a great bicycle
It's white and red
but my favourite thing
of all is sleeping in bed!

Chorus

Activity:

Are these sentences true or false?

a Gemma's got short brown hair.
b Gemma likes sport.
c Gemma can play the violin.
d Gemma likes watching TV.
e Gemma's got a purple bicycle.

Rock star

I make the bed every morning at eight
I tidy my room and put on my roller skates
I skate to school five days a week
I do my homework in the evening and I clean
my teeth

Monday to Friday, I work and do my chores
I read my books and I clean the floors
But at the weekends, I sing and play the guitar
because I'm a famous rock star

Chorus
  It's the weekend now and I'm singing, I'm dancing
  I'm writing songs and having fun
  It's the weekend now and I'm singing, I'm dancing
  I'm singing my song, it's number one!

I eat my lunch at school with my mates
A cheese salad sandwich and a piece of cake
We take the bus home and we hang out after school
My friends don't know my secret, and that is cool

Yes, on Saturday and Sunday I don't work,
or do my chores
I don't read my books or clean the floors
Because I'm a world famous rock star
And at the weekends, I sing and play the guitar

Chorus

Activity:

When does the Rock star do these things?
Write *Monday to Friday* or *Weekend*.

a do homework _____
b clean the floor _____
c play the guitar _____
d write songs _____
e dance _____
f eat a cheese and salad sandwich _____

Module 3, Lesson 10, Activity 6

Our family

I'm the best with computers
I'm really good at IT
My cousin Joe is the sportiest
He loves to do PE
My uncle Fred's the most-generous
He buys presents as big as a house.
My brother Mike's the most talkative
He loves chatting, even to a mouse!

Chorus
  Welcome to our family
  We're the friendliest people in town
  Welcome to our family
  We're the happiest people around

My mum is the most hard-working
She's always got things to do
My great-grandma is the oldest
She's one hundred and two
My cousin Jen's the youngest
She's only one and a half
My sister Sue is the funniest
She makes everybody laugh

Chorus

Activity:
Who is …

a very sporty   _____
b very talkative   _____
c very hard-working   _____
d very old   _____
e very young   _____
f very funny   _____

Module 4, Lesson 14, Activity 5

Dream Park

Chorus
  We've got our own rules, in our dream park
  Life's pretty cool, in our dream park
  We can have a great time, in our dream park
  We're always fine, in our dream park

You can lie on the grass
You can jump and sing
You can wear roller-skates
You can do anything
But you have to have fun
in the rain, in the sun
in our Dream Park
in our Dream Park

You can ride your bikes
You can swim in the lake
You can drink cola
and eat chocolate cake
But you have to have fun
in the rain, in the sun
in our Dream Park
in our Dream Park

Chorus

You can kick a ball
You can climb the trees
You can fly a kite
You can do as you please
But you have to have fun
in the rain, in the sun
in our Dream Park
in our Dream Park

Chorus

Activity:
Find the rhyming words in the song:

a anything   _____
b sun   _____
c cake   _____
d please   _____

Last summer

Last summer we went to the mountains
and then we took the fast train to Rome
Last summer we travelled to Paris
and then we cycled all the way home

Chorus
  Now it is winter
  The sky is cold and grey
  But I remember last summer
  I had fun every day.

Last summer we listened to music
and then we swam in the sea
Last summer, we danced on the beach
Last summer, oh yes, we were free

Chorus

Last summer, we sang songs together
and then we played volleyball in the park
Last summer, we camped on the beach
Last summer we counted the stars in the dark

Chorus

Activity:
Find and write the past simple form of these verbs:

a take _____
b swim _____
c sing _____
d play _____
e count _____

Gulliver's story

Chorus
  Listen, will you listen
  to this story of mine
  When I was a ship's doctor
  in sixteen ninety-nine

My ship hit a rock
in a terrible storm
I swam to an island
and I slept until dawn*

I woke on a beach
and saw a very small man
I spoke to him in English
He did not understand

There were hundreds of soldiers
on the beach, by the sea
They were tiny but dangerous
and they shot arrows at me

I was hungry and thirsty
I wanted to eat
and so the soldiers fed me
then I slept on the beach

A thousand horses pulled a wagon
and I travelled in the night
To a beautiful city
with a palace, fine and bright

Chorus

dawn = when the sun rises in the morning

Activity:
Find words in the song to match these definitions.

a very bad
b bad weather with rain and wind
c very small
d when you want to eat food
e when you want to drink water
f a big building for a king or queen

Let's go to Funland!

I want to visit Funland
I want to ride the rollercoasters with you [too scary!]
I want to eat hot dogs and ice cream
and go horse-riding with you

Chorus
  I want to have some fun
  How about you?
  Yes, let's have some fun
  Let's go to Funland, me and you

I want to visit Funland
I want to go rafting with you [too cold!]
I want to have a picnic
and sit in the park with you.

Chorus

I want to visit Funland
I want to go to the Haunted castle with you [Let's go!]
I want to take a lot of photos
and have a lot of fun with you

Chorus

Activity:

What does the singer want to do? Find words in the song to complete these sentences.

The singer wants to:

a ride the _____ in F_____ .
b eat _____ and _____ .
c go r_____
d have a p_____ in the p_____ .
e go to the H_____ c_____ .

Grammar summary

❶ Present tense verb *be*

- Notice how we use the present tense verb *be*:

Are you Teresa?

No, I'm not. I'm Tina. She's Teresa.

Affirmative sentences:

Full form	Short form
I **am** friendly.	I'm friendly.
You **are** friendly.	You're friendly.
He **is**	He's
She **is** friendly.	She's friendly.
It **is**	It's
We **are**	We're
You **are** friendly.	You're friendly.
They **are**	They're

Negative sentences:

Full form	Short form
I **am not** friendly.	I'm **not** friendly.
You **are not**	You **aren't**
He **is not**	He **isn't**
She **is not** friendly.	She **isn't** friendly.
It **is not**	It **isn't**
We **are not**	We **aren't**
You **are not** friendly.	You **aren't** friendly.
They **are not**	They **aren't**

Questions and short answers:

Question	Short answer
Am I friendly?	Yes, I **am.**/No, I'm **not.**
Are you friendly?	Yes, you **are.**/No, you **aren't.**
Is he	Yes, he **is.**/No, he **isn't.**
Is she friendly?	Yes, she **is.**/No, she **isn't.**
Is it	Yes, it **is.**/No, it **isn't.**
Are we	Yes, we **are.**/No, we **aren't.**
Are you friendly?	Yes, you **are.**/No, you **aren't.**
Are they	Yes, they **are.**/No, they **aren't.**

Check your grammar

Complete the questions with *is* or *are*. Write true answers.

1 Is pizza your favourite food?   No, it isn't.

1. pizza/your favourite food?
2. your shoes/new?
3. your birthday/in June?
4. you/twelve years old?
5. your friends/twelve years old?

❷ *Have got*

- Notice how we use *have got*:

Has she got straight hair?

No, she **hasn't**. She's **got** curly hair.

Affirmative sentences:

Full form	Short form
I **have got** a cat.	I've **got** a cat.
You **have got** a cat.	You've **got** a cat.
He **has got**	He's **got**
She **has got** a cat.	She's **got** a cat.
It **has got**	It's **got**
We **have got**	We've **got**
You **have got** a cat.	You've **got** a cat.
They **have got**	They've **got**

Negative sentences:

Full form	Short form
I **have not got** a cat.	I **haven't got** a cat.
You **have not got** a cat.	You **haven't got** a cat.
He **has not got**	He **hasn't got**
She **has not got** a cat.	She **hasn't got** a cat.
It **has not got**	It **hasn't got**
We **have not got**	We **haven't got**
You **have not got** a cat.	You **haven't got** a cat.
They **have not got**	They **haven't got**

Questions and short answers:

Question	Short answer
Have I **got** a cat?	Yes, I **have**./ No, I **haven't**.
Have you **got** a cat?	Yes, you **have**./ No, you **haven't**.
Has he **got** **Has** she **got** a cat? **Has** it **got**	Yes, he/she/it **has**. No, he/she/it **hasn't**.
Have we **got** **Have** you **got** a cat? **Have** they **got**	Yes, we/you/they **have**. No, we/you/they **haven't**.

Check your grammar

Make true sentences about you and your classmate with: *I've got …/I haven't got … My classmate has got …/hasn't got …*

1 I've got straight hair. My classmate hasn't got straight hair.

1 straight hair
2 brown eyes
3 long hair
4 two sisters
5 a bike

❸ Present simple

- Notice how we use the present simple:

Does he **play** football and tennis?

He **plays** football but he **doesn't play** tennis.

Affirmative sentences:

Singular	Plural
I **play** football. You **play** football.	We **play** football. You **play** football.
He **plays** She **plays** football. It **plays**	They **play** football.

Negative sentences:

Full form	Short form
I **do not play** tennis.	I **don't play** tennis.
You **do not play** tennis.	You **don't** play tennis.
He **does not** She **does not play** tennis. It **does not**	He **doesn't** She **doesn't play** tennis. It **doesn't**
We **do not** You **do not** **play** tennis. They **do not**	We **don't** You **don't** **play** tennis. They **don't**

Questions and short answers:

Question	Short answer
Do I **play** tennis?	Yes, I **do**. No, I **don't**.
Do you **play** tennis?	Yes, you **do**. No, you **don't**.
Does he **Does** she **play** tennis? **Does** it	Yes, he/she/it **does**. No, he/she/it **doesn't**.
Do we **Do** you **play** tennis? **Do** they	Yes, we/you/they **do**. No, we/you/they **don't**.

Check your grammar

Choose the correct words.

1 Do you like Maths? Yes, I do.

1 **A:** *Do/Does* you *like/likes* Maths?
   B: Yes, I *do/does*.
2 **A:** *Do/Does* your best friend *like/likes* Maths?
   B: No, she *don't/doesn't*. She *like/likes* English.
3 **A:** Where *do/does* you live?
   B: I *live/lives* in Brighton.
4 Mary *don't/doesn't* like sport.
5 We *watch/watches* soaps on TV but we don't watch the news.
6 **A:** *Do/Does* they wear trainers?
   B: Yes, they *do/does*.

❹ Can (ability)

- Notice how we use *can* to talk about ability:

Can you ski?

I **can** ski, but I **can't** ice-skate.

Affirmative sentences:

Singular	Plural
I **can** ski.	We **can** ski.
You **can** ski.	You **can** ski.
He **can**	
She **can** ski.	They **can** ski.
It **can**	

Negative sentences:

Full form	Short form
I **cannot** ski.	I **can't** ski.
You **cannot** ski.	You **can't** ski.
He **cannot**	He **can't**
She **cannot** ski.	She **can't** ski.
It **cannot**	It **can't**
We **cannot**	We **can't**
You **cannot** ski.	You **can't** ski.
They **cannot**	They **can't**

Questions and short answers:

Question	Short answer
Can I ski?	Yes, I **can**./ No, I **can't**.
Can you ski?	Yes, you **can**./No, you **can't**.
Can he **Can** she ski? **Can** it	Yes, he/she/it **can**. No, he/she/it **can't**.
Can we **Can** you ski? **Can** they	Yes, we/you/they **can**. No, we/you/they **can't**.

Check your grammar

Look at the pictures. Make sentences about these children with *He/She can/can't* …

1   He can't ski.

❺ Present continuous

- Notice how we use the present continuous.

Are you **doing** the washing up?

No, I'm **not**. I'm **vacuuming** the carpet.

Affirmative sentences:

Full form	Short form
I **am eating**.	I'm **eating**.
You **are eating**.	You're **eating**.
He **is**	He's
She **is** **eating**.	She's **eating**.
It **is**	It's
We **are**	We're
You **are** **eating**.	You're **eating**.
They **are**	They're

Negative Sentences:

Full form	Short form
I **am not eating**.	I**'m not eating**.
You **are not eating**.	You **aren't eating**.
He **is not**	He **isn't**
She **is not** eating.	She **isn't** eating.
It **is not**	It **isn't**
We **are not**	We **aren't**
You **are not** eating.	You **aren't** eating.
They **are not**	They **aren't**

Questions and short answers:

Question	Short answer
Am I	Yes, I **am**./No, I**'m not**.
Are you	Yes, you **are**./No, you**'re not**.
Is he	
Is she eating?	Yes, he/she/it **is**.
Is it	No, he/she/it **isn't**.
Are we	
Are you	Yes, we/you/they **are**.
Are they	No, we/you/they **aren't**.

Check your grammar

Complete the questions with the present continuous. Write true answers.

1 Are you sitting in the classroom? Yes, I am.

1 you/sit/in the classroom?
2 you/wear/jeans?
3 you/sit/near the window?
4 it/rain?
5 you/study/English?
6 your classmate/read?

❻ Adverbs and expressions of frequency

Expressions of frequency

- Notice how we use expressions of frequency:

Do you go swimming **every day**?

No, I don't. I usually go **twice a week**.

- Notice the word order

We go shopping **two or three times a month**.
Do you watch TV **every day**?

Adverbs of frequency

- Notice how we use adverbs of frequency:

How **often** do you walk to school?

I **never** walk to school. I **always** take the bus.

- Notice the word order:

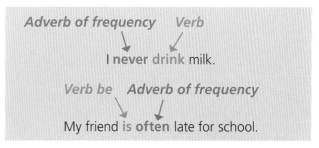

Adverb of frequency   Verb

I **never drink** milk.

Verb be   Adverb of frequency

My friend **is often** late for school.

Check your grammar

Make questions with these words. Then answer the questions about you.

1 Do you always get up early?
No, I don't. I usually get up late on Saturday.

1 Do you/early/get up/always/?
2 Are you/in the morning/tired/?
3 Do you/every weekend/shopping/go/?
4 Do you/often/to the cinema/go/?
5 Are you/at home/usually/?
6 Do you/your friends/every day/meet/?

❼ Present simple and present continuous

Present simple

- Notice how we use the present simple:

Do you often **play** computer games?

Yes, I **do**.

Present continuous

- Notice how we use the present continuous:

What game **are** you **playing**?

I**'m playing** The Maze.

Check your grammar

Choose the correct words.

1 It's *raining/rains*.

2 Yes, I *play/I'm playing* tennis.

3 I usually *go/I'm going* to bed at 10.30.

4 I *go/I'm going* to bed. Good night.

❽ Comparative and superlative adjectives

Comparative

- Notice how we use comparative adjectives:

You are **taller** than me.

You are **more hard-working** than me.

Superlative

- Notice how we use superlative adjectives.

You are **the tallest**.

You are the **most hard-working**.

Short adjectives:

Adjective	Comparative	Superlative
tall	tall**er**	tall**est**
old	old**er**	old**est**

Short adjectives ending in a vowel + a consonant:

Adjective	Comparative	Superlative
big	big**ger**	big**gest**
fit	fit**ter**	fit**test**

Short adjectives ending in a y:

Adjective	Comparative	Superlative
funny	funn**ier**	funn**iest**
happy	happ**ier**	happ**iest**

Longer adjectives:

Adjective	Comparative	Superlative
comfortable	**more** comfortable	**most** comfortable
talkative	**more** talkative	**most** talkative

Irregular adjectives:

Adjective	Comparative	Superlative
good	better	best
bad	worse	worst

Check your grammar

Complete with the comparative form of the adjective in brackets.

1   I'm older than my brother.

1   I'm _____ than my brother. (old)
2   I think my sister is _____ than me. (talkative)
3   I think my brother is _____ than me. (friendly)
4   My sister is _____ than me. (funny)
5   I'm _____ than my brother. (tall)

Check your grammar

a) Write six questions with *What/Who is the … in our country*? Use the superlative form and these words:

1   What is the biggest city in our country?

1   big city
2   high mountain
3   expensive car
4   good singer
5   important person
6   long river

b) Then answer the questions.

1   Moscow is the biggest city in our country.

❾ Object pronouns

- Notice how we use object pronouns.

You're fitter than **me**.

Do you like **it**?

- The object pronouns are:

Singular	Plural
me	us
you	you
him	
her	them
it	

Check your grammar

Complete with *me, him, her, it, us, them.*

1   Look at them.

Look at _____ .

Look at _____ .

Look at _____ .

Look at _____ .

Look at _____ .

Look at _____ .

Look at _____ .

Check your grammar

Complete the text with *me, him, her, it, us, them.*

My name is Steve. I have got one brother and one sister. My sister's name is Liza and my brother's name is Edward. Liza is 15 and I'm 12. She is older than _____ . She is very nice and I like _____ a lot. Edward is ten. I'm older than _____ . My grandmother also lives at home with _____ . I like music very much and play the piano but I can't play _____ very well. My top two sports are basketball and football and I like _____ very much.

❿ *Have to* (obligation)

- Notice how we use *have to* to talk about obligation.

Affirmative sentences:

Singular	Plural
I **have to go** shopping.	We **have to go** shopping.
You **have to go** shopping.	You **have to go** shopping.
He **has to go** She **has to go** shopping. It **has to go**	They **have to go** shopping.

Negative sentences:

Full form	Short form
I **do not have to go**.	I **don't have to go**.
You **do not have to go**.	You **don't have to go**.
He **does** She **does not have to go**. It **does not**	He **doesn't** She **doesn't have to go**. It **doesn't**
We **do not** You **do not have to go**. They **do not**	We **don't** You **don't have to go**. They **don't**

Questions and short answers:

Question	Short answer
Do I **have to go**?	Yes, I **do**./No, I **don't**.
Do you **have to go**?	Yes, you **do**./No. you **don't**.
Does he **Does** she **have to go**? **Does** it	No, he/she/it **doesn't**. Yes, he/she/it **does**.
Do we **Do** you **have to go**? **Do** they	Yes, we/you/they **do**. No, we/you/they **don't**.

Check your grammar

a) Look at Jane's list. Complete the sentences with *has to* or *doesn't have to*.

1 Jane doesn't have to wear a school uniform.

1 Jane _____ wear a school uniform.
2 She _____ do homework.
3 She _____ study German.
4 She _____ start school at half past eight.
5 She _____ go to school at the weekend.
6 She _____ do tests.

b) Then make true sentences about yourself.

1 I don't have to wear school uniform.

⓫ *Can* (permission/requests)

- Notice how we use *can* to ask and give permission:

Check your grammar

What can you do at your school? Make true sentences with We can… /We can't …

1 *We can't eat in the classroom.*

1 eat in the classroom
2 have lunch at school
3 sit with friends
4 drink water in the classroom
5 speak to classmates in the classroom

⑫ Countable and uncountable nouns

- Notice these countable and uncountable nouns.

Countable		Uncountable	
an egg		rice	
a boy		hair	
two coins		money	

- Countable nouns have plural forms. They can be counted.

(One egg, two eggs, three eggs, four eggs …)

- Uncountable nouns don't have plural forms. They can't be counted.

  You *can't* say: rices.
  You *can't* say: one rice, two rice, etc.

- We have to use *a*, *an*, *one*, *the*, *my*, etc. with singular countable nouns.

(I've got **an** egg.)

- We can use *some*, *any* and *a lot of* with plural countable *and* uncountable nouns.

(I've got **some** money.)

(He's got **a lot of** money.)

(Are there **any** eggs?)

(We have **a lot of** eggs.)

- Notice how we use *how much* and *how many*

How much + uncountable noun

(**How much money** have you got?)

How many + countable noun

(**How many eggs** have you got?)

Check your grammar

Choose the correct words and complete the sentences.

1 *Is the milk cold?*

1 *Is/Are* the ____ cold?

2 Where *is/are* my ____?

3 Your ____ *is/are* beautiful.

4 *Is/Are* this your ____?

5 How *much/many* ____ have you got?

6 How *much/many* ____ have you got?

(101)

⑬ Past tense verb *be*

- Notice how we use the past tense verb *be*:

Who **was** Cleopatra?

She **was** an Egyptian queen.

Where **were** you last night?

We **were** at home.

Affirmative sentences:

Singular	Plural
I **was** at home.	We **were** at home.
You **were** at home.	You **were** at home.
He **was** She **was** at home. It **was**	They **were** at home.

Negative sentences:

Full form	Short form
I **was not** at home.	I **wasn't** at home.
You **were not** at home.	You **weren't** at home.
He **was not** She **was not** at home. It **was not**	He **wasn't** She **wasn't** at home. It **wasn't**
We **were not** You **were not** at home. They **were not**	We **weren't** You **weren't** at home. They **weren't**

Questions and short answers:

Question	Short answer
Was I at home?	Yes, I **was**./No. I **wasn't**.
Were you at home?	Yes, you **were**./No, you **weren't**.
Was he	Yes, he **was**./No, he **wasn't**.
Was she at home?	Yes, she **was**./No, she **wasn't**.
Was it	Yes, it **was**./No, it **wasn't**.
Were we	Yes, we **were**./No, we **weren't**.
Were you at home?	Yes, you **were**./No, you **weren't**.
Were they	Yes, they **were**./No, they **weren't**.

Check your grammar

Complete with *was*, *wasn't*, *were* or *weren't*.

1   Were you late for school this morning?

1 A:_____ you late for school this morning?
B: No, I _____. I _____ on time.
2 A:_____ all the students there?
B: No, they _____. Two students _____ late.
3 A:_____ your teacher happy?
B: No, she _____. She _____ very angry.

⑭ Past simple

- Notice how we use the past simple:

Did you **play** volleyball last weekend?

No, I **didn't**. I **played** football.

I **went** to bed early last night.

I **didn't go** to bed early last Friday.

- Notice some past simple verbs are regular and some are irregular:

Regular	Irregular
play > **played**	go > **went**
watch > **watched**	sit > **sat**
cycle > **cycled**	read > **read**

- See the irregular verb list on page 105.

Affirmative sentences:

Singular	Plural
I **played** football.	We **played** football.
You **played** football.	You **played** football.
He	
She **played** football.	They **played** football.
It	

Negative sentences:

Full form	Short form
I **did not go** home.	I **didn't go** home.
You **did not go** home.	You **didn't go** home.
He	He
She **did not** go home.	She **didn't go home**.
It	It
We	We
You **did not go** home.	You **didn't go** home.
They	They

Questions and short answers:

Question	Short answer
Did I **play** football?	Yes, I **did**./No, I **didn't**.
Did you **play** football?	Yes, you **did**./No, you **didn't**.
he **Did** she **play** football? it	Yes, he/she/it **did**. No, he/she/it **didn't**.
we **Did** you **play** football? they	Yes, we/you/they **did**. No, we/you/they **didn't**.

Check your grammar

Copy and complete this list of regular verbs.

play	*played*	watch	_____
travel	_____	cycle	_____
ski	_____	phone	_____
use	_____		

Check your grammar

Copy and complete this list of irregular verbs.

take	*took*	have	_____
sit	_____	go	_____
read	_____	buy	_____
leave	_____	get	_____
see	_____		

Check your grammar

Sam always does the same thing every day. Read the text then write what he did **yesterday**.

7:30

He gets up at half past seven and he has a shower. Then he has breakfast. He leaves home at twenty past eight and walks to school. He arrives at school at a quarter to eight. He meets his friends after school. They play football. Then he goes home and watches TV. Then he does his homework. Then he reads a book and listens to music. Then he goes to bed.

He got up at half past seven and had a shower.
Then he ...

_____

_____

_____

_____

_____

_____

15 *There was, there were*

- Notice how we use *there was* and *there were*:

Were there many children at the party?

Yes, **there were.**

Was there any food at the party?

No, **there wasn't.**

Singular full form	Plural full form
There was some food.	**There were** many children.
There was not any food.	**There were not** many children.
Was there any food?	**Were there** many children?

Negative sentences short form:

Singular	Plural
There was some food.	**There were** many children.
There was not any food.	**There were not** many children.
Was there any food?	**Were there** many children?
No, **there wasn't**.	No, **there weren't.**

Check your grammar

Complete these sentences about this street with *there was*, *there wasn't*, *there were*, or *there weren't*.

1   *There wasn't a church.*

High Street, 1900

1 ____ a church.   4 ____ a café.
2 ____ some houses.   5 ____ trees.
3 ____ two shops.

16 *Going to* (plans/intentions)

- Notice how we use *going to* for plans and intentions:

Are you **going to watch** TV tonight?

No, **I'm not.**

I'm not going to watch TV tonight. I'm going to do my homework.

Affirmative Sentences:

Full form	Short form
I **am going to watch** TV.	**I'm going to watch** TV.
You **are going to watch** TV.	You**'re going to watch** TV.
He **is**	He**'s**
She **is going to watch** TV.	She**'s going to watch** TV.
It **is**	It**'s**
We **are**	We**'re going**
You **are going to watch** TV.	You**'re going to watch** TV.
They **are**	They**'re**

Negative Sentences:

Full form	Short form
I **am not going to play**.	**I'm not going to play**.
You **are not going to play**.	You **aren't going to play**.
He **is not**	He **isn't**
She **is not going to play**.	She **isn't going to play**.
It **is not**	It **isn't**
We **are not**	We **aren't**
You **are not going to play**.	You **aren't going to play**.
They **are not**	They **aren't**

Questions and short answers:

Question	Short answer
Am I **going to play**?	Yes, I **am**./No, **I'm not**.
Are you **going to play**?	Yes, you **are**./No, you **aren't**.
Is he	
Is she **going to play**?	Yes, he/she/it **is**.
Is it	No, he/she/it **isn't**.
Are we	
Are you **going to play**?	Yes, we/you/they **are**.
Are they	No, we/you/they **aren't**.

Check your grammar

How many of these things are you going to do tonight? Make sentences with *I'm going to … / I'm not going to …*

1 I'm going to watch TV.

1	watch TV	2	go to bed early
3	do some homework	4	tidy my room
5	read a book	6	play computer games

Past simple irregular verbs

Present simple	Past simple
be	was/were
become	became
begin	began
bring	brought
build	built
buy	bought
do	did
drink	drank
drive	drove
eat	ate
feed	fed
find	found
fly	flew
forget	forgot
get	got
go	went
hang out	hung out
have	had
hit	hit
learn	learnt
leave	left
make	made
meet	met
put on	put on
read	read
ride	rode
run	ran
see	saw
send	sent
shoot	shot
sit	sat
sleep	slept
speak	spoke
spend	spent
swim	swam
take	took
throw	threw
understand	understood
wake up	woke up
wear	wore
win	won
write	wrote

Wordlists

Module 1

Lesson 1

bike /baɪk/
famous /'feɪməs/
fantastic /fæn'tæstɪk/
flat /flæt/
football boots /'fʊtbɔːl ˌbuːts/
home /həʊm/
hometown /ˌhəʊm'taʊn/
hundred /'hʌndrəd/
Labrador /'læbrəˌdɔː/
million /'mɪljən/
muddy /'mʌdi/
ordinal number /ˌɔːdɪnl 'nʌmbə/
  first /fɜːst/
  second /'sekənd/
  third /θɜːd/
  fourth /fɔːθ/
  fifth /fɪfθ/
  sixth /sɪksθ/
  seventh /'sevnθ/
  eighth /eɪtθ/
  ninth /naɪnθ/
  tenth /tenθ/
  eleventh /ɪ'levnθ/
  twelfth /twelfθ/
  thirteenth /ˌθɜː'tiːnθ/
  fourteenth /ˌfɔː'tiːnθ/
  fifteenth /ˌfɪf'tiːnθ/
  sixteenth /ˌsiks'tiːnθ/
  seventeenth /ˌsevn'tiːnθ/
  eighteenth /ˌeɪ'tiːnθ/
  nineteenth /ˌnaɪn'tiːnθ/
  twentieth /'twentiəθ/
  twenty-first /ˌtwenti 'fɜːst/
  thirtieth /'θɜːtiəθ/
pier /pɪə/
sea /siː/
sports mad /'spɔːts ˌmæd/
thousand /'θaʊznd/
world /'wɜːld/

Lesson 2

blonde hair /'blɒnd ˌheə/
blue eyes /'bluː ˌaɪz/
brown eyes /'braʊn ˌaɪz/
curly /'kɜːli/
dark brown hair /dɑːk 'braʊn ˌheə/
early /'ɜːli/
green eyes /'griːn ˌaɪz/
grey hair /'greɪ ˌheə/

hip hop /'hɪp ˌhɒp/
late /leɪt/
light brown hair /laɪt 'braʊn ˌheə/
long /'lɒŋ/
medium-length /'miːdiəm ˌleŋθ/
poem /'pəʊɪm/
quite /kwaɪt/
short /ʃɔːt/
skate (v) /skeɪt/
soap (soap opera) /səʊp ['səʊp ˌɒprə]/
straight /streɪt/
trainers /'treɪnəz/
the news /ˌðə 'njuːz/
water-ski /'wɔːtəˌskiː/
wavy /'weɪvi/

Lesson 3

carrots /'kærət/
cartwheel /'kɑːtˌwiːl/
ears /'ɪəs/
e-pal /'iːpæl/
getting up early /ˌgetɪŋ ʌp 'ɜːli/
hanging out /'hæŋɪŋ ˌaʊt/
keyboards /'kiːˌbɔːrdz/
kilometre /'kɪləˌmɪtə/
meat /miːt/
music /'mjuːzɪk/
New Zealand /ˌnjuː 'ziːlənd/
purple /'pɜːpl/
revising (for tests) /rɪ'vaɪzɪŋ [fə tests]/
Shetland Islands /ˌʃetlənd 'aɪləndz/
sailing /'seɪlɪŋ/
vegetarian /ˌvedʒə'teəriən/
wiggle /'wɪgl/

Lesson 4

air-conditioning /'eə kənˌdɪʃnɪŋ/
Asia /'eɪʃə/
Chinese /ˌtʃaɪ'niːz/
chopsticks /'tʃɒpˌstɪks/
cricket /'krɪkɪt/
equator /ɪ'kweɪtə/
floor (of a building) /flɔː/
fork /fɔːk/
high-rise building /'haɪraɪz ˌbɪldɪŋ/
humid /'hjuːmɪd/
knife /naɪf/
Malay /mə'leɪ/
Maori /'maʊri/
noodles /'nuːdlz/
official /ə'fɪʃl/

rugby /'rʌgbi/
Singapore /ˌsɪŋə'pɔː/
speak /spiːk/
southeast /ˌsaʊθ'iːst/
Tamil /'tæmɪl/
vegetables /'vedʒtəblz/
water sport /'wɔːtəˌspɔːt/

Module 1 Extra Special

American football /əˌmerɪkən 'fʊtbɔːl/
Argentina /ˌɑːdʒən'tiːnə/
baseball /'beɪsˌbɔːl/
basketball /'bɑːskɪtˌbɔːl/
Brazil /brə'zɪl/
California /ˌkælɪ'fɔːnɪə/
Canada /'kænədə/
capital (city) /ˌkæpɪtl ['sɪti]/
cell phone /'sel ˌfəʊn/
cookie /'kʊki/
Cuba /'kjuːbə/
eraser /ɪ'reɪzə/
Florida /'flɒrɪdə/
happiness /'hæpɪnəs/
liberty /'lɪbəti/
Mexico /'meksɪˌkəʊ/
moon /muːn/
pants /pænts/
popular /'pɒpjʊlə/
president /'prezɪdənt/
sneakers /'sniːkəz/
statue /'stætʃuː/
Texas /'teksəs/
trash /træʃ/

Module 2

Lesson 5

bin /bɪn/
carpet /'kɑːpɪt/
do /duː/
empty (v) /'empti/
feed /fiːd/
fish (n) /fɪʃ/
go /gəʊ/
make /meɪk/
raincoat /'reɪnˌkəʊt/
roller skates /'rəʊlə ˌskeɪts/
rubber gloves /ˌrʌbə 'glʌvz/
take /teɪk/
tidy /'taɪdi/
toothbrush /'tuːθˌbrʌʃ/
toys /tɔɪz/
vacuum /'vækjʊəm/
wash /wɒʃ/

Lesson 6

afternoon /ˌɑːftə'nuːn/
always /'ɔːlweɪz/
evening /'iːvnɪŋ/
every /'evri/
frequency /'friːkwənsi/
how often /ˌhaʊ 'ɒfn/
morning /'mɔːnɪŋ/
never /'nevə/
night /naɪt/
once /wʌns/
snack /snæk/
sometimes /'sʌmtaɪmz/
twice /twaɪs/
usually /'juːʒʊəli/

Lesson 7

bottle /'bɒtl/
box /bɒks/
can (n) /kæn/
cardboard /'kɑːdˌbɔːd/
cook (profession) /kʊk/
glass /glɑːs/
it /ɪt/
jar /dʒɑː/
lorry /'lɒri/
made (of) /meɪd [əv]/
metal /'metl/
packet /'pækɪt/
paper /'peɪpə/
plastic /'plæstɪk/
pot /pɒt/
recycle /riː'saɪkl/
secretary /'sekrətri/
them /ðem/
wrapper /'ræpə/

Lesson 8

bacon /'beɪkən/
beans /'biːnz/
B&B (Bed and Breakfast)
    /ˌbiː ən 'biː [ˌbed ən 'brekfəst]/
collect /kə'lekt/
eggs /egz/
fetch /fetʃ/
guest /gest/
mushroom /'mʌʃruːm/
sausage /'sɒsɪdʒ/
school holiday /ˌskuːl 'hɒlɪdeɪ/
shake (v) /ʃeɪk/
sweep /swiːp/
tomato /tə'mɑːtəʊ/
well (n) /wel/
wood /wʊd/

Module 2 Extra special

expensive /ɪkˈspensɪv/
heavy /ˈhevi/
invent /ɪnˈvent/
leather /ˈleðə/
measure (v) /ˈmeʒə/
sugar /ˈʃʊgə/

Module 3

Lesson 9

better /ˈbetə/
bigger /ˈbɪgə/
comfortable /ˈkʌmftəbl/
comparative /kəmˈpærətɪv/
compare /kəmˈpeə/
funnier /ˈfʌniə/
friendlier /ˈfrendliə/
friendly /ˈfrendli/
funny /ˈfʌni/
good at sport /gʊd ət ˈspɔːt/
hard-working /ˌhɑːdˈwɜːkɪŋ/
her /hɜː/
him /hɪm/
longer /ˈlɒŋə/
me /miː/
older /ˈəʊldə/
shorter /ˈʃɔːtə/
smaller /ˈsmɔːlə/
talkative /ˈtɔːkətɪv/
taller /ˈtɔːlə/
tall /tɔːl/
them /ðem/
us /ʌs/
you /juː/
younger /ˈjʌŋgə/

Lesson 10

best /best/
chatting /ˈtʃætɪŋ/
crazy about /ˌkreɪzi əˈbaʊt/
fittest /ˈfɪtest/
generous /ˈdʒenərəs/
gym /dʒɪm/
handsome /ˈhænsm/
messiest /ˈmesiest/
superlative /sʊˈpɜːlətɪv/
youngest /ˈjʌŋgest/

Lesson 11

animal /ˈænɪml/
ant /ænt/
bear /beə/
bragger /ˈbrægə/
buffalo /ˈbʌfələʊ/

camel /ˈkæml/
cheetah /ˈtʃiːtə/
chimpanzee /ˌtʃɪmpænˈziː/
cobra /ˈkəʊbrə/
dangerous /ˈdeɪndʒərəs/
deer /dɪə/
dog /dɒg/
dolphin /ˈdɒlfɪn/
elephant /ˈelɪfənt/
fast /fɑːst/
fly /flaɪ/
horse /hɔːs/
hotdogs /ˈhɒtˌdɒgz/
intelligent /ɪnˈtelɪdʒnt/
mosquito /mɒˈskiːtəʊ/
mouse /maʊs/
owl /aʊl/
polite /pəˈlaɪt/
scorpion /ˈskɔːpiən/
snail /sneɪl/
strong /strɒŋ/
tortoise /ˈtɔːtəs/

Lesson 12

also /ˈɔːlsəʊ/
beautiful /ˈbjuːtəfl/
big /bɪg/
boring /ˈbɔːrɪŋ/
comfortable /ˈkʌmftəbl/
dark /dɑːk/
exciting /ɪkˈsaɪtɪŋ/
expensive /ɪkˈspensɪv/
fit /fɪt/
friendly /ˈfrendli/
fun /fʌn/
funny /ˈfʌni/
generous /ˈdʒenərəs/
good /gʊd/
hard-working /ˌhɑːdˈwɜːkɪŋ/
however /haʊˈevə/
interesting /ˈɪntrəstɪŋ/
long /lɒŋ/
messy /ˈmesi/
old /əʊld/
polite /pəˈlaɪt/
short /ʃɔːt/
small /smɔːl/
talkative /ˈtɔːkətɪv/
tall /tɔːl/
village /ˈvɪlɪdʒ/
young /jʌŋ/

Module 3 – Extra Special

Barbados /bɑːˈbeɪdəʊs/
crazy /ˈkreɪzi/
fashion designer /ˈfæʃn dɪˌzaɪnə/
songwriter /ˈsɒŋˌraɪtə/

108

successful /sək'sesfl/
surfing /'sɜːfɪŋ/

Module 4

Lesson 13

bow (v) /baʊ/
greet /griːt/
heavy /'hevi/
jacket /'dʒækɪt/
lesson /'lesn/
put hand up /'pʊt ˌhænd ʌp/
slippers /'slɪpəz/
switch off /ˌswɪtʃ 'ɒf/
tie (n) /taɪ/
uniform /'juːnɪˌfɔːm/

Lesson 14

basketball /'baːskɪtˌbɔːl/
bowling /'bəʊlɪŋ/
carry /'kæri/
catch /kætʃ/
football /'fʊtbɔːl/
gloves /glʌvz/
goalkeeper /'gəʊlˌkiːpə/
head (a ball) /hed [ə bɔːl]/
helmet /'helmɪt/
hit /hɪt/
ice hockey /ˌaɪs ˌhɒki/
kick /kɪk/
hold /həʊld/
net /net/
puck /pʌk/
racket /'rækɪt/
roll (v) /rəʊl/
rule /ruːl/
sweatband /'swetˌbænd/
tennis /'tenɪs/
throw /θrəʊ/

Lesson 15

a lot of /ə 'lɒt ˌɒv/
apples /'æpls/
bananas /bə'naːnəz/
biscuits /'bɪskɪt/
bread /bred/
cheese /tʃiːz/
chicken /'tʃɪkɪn/
cola /'kəʊlə/
countable /'kaʊntəbl/
diet /daɪət/
fish /fɪʃ/
many /'meni/
meat /miːt/
milk /mɪlk/
much /mʌtʃ/

oranges /'ɒrɪndʒs/
pasta /'pæstə/
potatoes /pə'teɪtəʊz/
rice /raɪs/
salad /'sæləd/
salt /sɔːlt/
sugar /'ʃʊgə/
tomatoes /tə'maːtəʊz/
uncountable /ʌn'kaʊntəbl/
waiter /'weɪtə/

Lesson 16

back /bæk/
bare feet /'beə ˌfiːt/
beach volleyball /'biːtʃ ˌvɒlibɔːl/
fussy /'fʌsi/
ground /graʊnd/
pass /paːs/
serve (the ball) /sɜːv [ðə bɔːl]/
strict /strɪkt/
textbook /'tekstˌbʊk/
touch /tʌtʃ/

Module 4 Extra Special

athletics /æθ'letɪks/
Argentina /ˌaːdʒən'tiːnə/
Austria /'ɒstrɪə/
baseball /'beɪsˌbɔːl/
classical (music) /ˌklæsɪkl 'mjuːzɪk/
fencing /'fensɪŋ/
flamenco /flə'meŋkəʊ/
golf /gɒlf/
harp /haːp/
high jump /'haɪ ˌdʒʌmp/
long jump /'lɒŋ ˌdʒʌmp/
marathon /'mærəθn/
match (football match) /mætʃ ['fʊtbɔːl ˌmætʃ]/
modern /'mɒdən/
players (on a team) /'pleɪəz [ɒn ə tiːm]/
pole vault /'pəʊl ˌvɔːlt/
rugby /'rʌgbi/
samba /'sæmbə/
snow boarding /'snəʊˌbɔːɪŋ/
table tennis /'teɪbl ˌtenɪs/
tango /'tæŋgəʊ/
waltz /wɔːls/

Module 5

Lesson 17

American /ə'merɪkən/
astronomer /ə'strɒnəmə/
athlete /'æθliːt/
artist /'aːtɪst/
composer /kəm'pəʊzə/
dancer /'daːnsə/

discovery /dɪ'skʌvri/
Egyptian /ɪ'dʒɪpʃən/
English /'ɪŋglɪʃ/
film-star /'fɪlm ˌstɑː/
French /frentʃ/
German /'dʒɜːmən/
inventor /ɪn'ventə/
Italian /ɪ'tæljən/
musician /mju'zɪʃn/
nationality /ˌnæʃə'næləti/
occupation /ˌɒkjʊ'peɪʃn/
painting (n) /'peɪntɪŋ/
Polish /'pəʊlɪʃ/
popular /'pɒpjʊlə/
queen /kwiːn/
radium /'reɪdiəm/
Russian /'rʌʃn/
scientist /'saɪəntɪst/
singer /'sɪŋə/
Spanish /'spænɪʃ/
teacher /'tiːtʃə/
writer /'raɪtə/

Lesson 18

cycle /'saɪkl/
microwave /'maɪkrəˌweɪv/
mountain /'maʊntɪn/
past (n) /pɑːst/
ski /skiː/
space (outer space) /speɪs [ˌaʊtə 'speɪs]/
travel (v) /'trævl/

Lesson 19

bench /bentʃ/
grass /grɑːs/
lie (n) /laɪ/
magazine /ˌmægə'ziːn/
newspaper /'njuːzˌpeɪpə/
play (theatre) /'pleɪ ['θɪərə]/
statement /'steɪtmənt/
taxi /'tæksi/
true /truː/
truth /truːθ/
underground (subway/train/metro)
    /ˌʌndə'graʊnd ['sʌbˌweɪ/treɪn/'metrəʊ]/
yesterday /'jestədeɪ/

Lesson 20

above /ə'bʌv/
alibi /'ælɪbaɪ/
amazing /ə'meɪzɪŋ/
beefeater /'biːfˌiːtə/
boat trip /'bəʊt ˌtrɪp/
brilliant /'brɪljənt/
coach [bus] /kəʊtʃ [bʌs]/
diary /'daɪəri/

dinosaur /'daɪnəˌsɔː/
enormous /ɪ'nɔːməs/
fantastic /fæn'tæstɪk/
hostel /hɒstl/
interesting /'ɪntrəstɪŋ/
jewel /'dʒuːəl/
lift /lɪft/
on the way /ɒn ði: weɪ/
statement /'steɪtmənt/
steps /steps/
tower /'taʊə/
traffic /'træfɪk/
view (n) /vjuː/

Module 5 Extra Special

by heart /ˌbaɪ 'hɑːt/
cheap /tʃiːp/
limousine /ˌlɪmə'ziːn/
lucky /'lʌki/
sell /sel/
title /'taɪtl/
What's happening? /'wɒts ˌhæpnɪŋ/

Module 6

Lesson 21

arrive /ə'raɪv/
cereal /'sɪəriəl/
comb (v) /kəʊm/
forget /fə'get/
pick up /ˌpɪk 'ʌp/
put on /ˌpʊt 'ɒn/
wake up /ˌweɪk 'ʌp/

Lesson 22

beach /biːtʃ/
café /'kæfeɪ/
donkey /'dɒŋki/
fishermen /'fɪʃəmen/
last night /ˌlɑːst 'naɪt/
last summer /ˌlɑːst 'sʌmə/
last weekend /ˌlɑːst 'wiːkend/
postcard /'pəʊstˌkɑːd/
sandcastle /'sændˌkɑːsl/
sea /siː/
seaside /' siːˌsaɪd/
shade /ʃeɪd/
wetsuit /'wetˌsuːt/

Lesson 23

arrow /'ærəʊ/
bow (and arrow) /bəʊ [ənd 'ærəʊ]/
centimetre /'sentɪˌmiːtə/
children /'tʃɪldrən/

doctor /ˈdɒktə/
horse /hɔːs/
huge /hjuːdʒ/
island /ˈaɪlənd/
palace /ˈpæləs/
point (v) /pɔɪnt/
rock /rɒk/
ship /ʃɪp/
shoot /ʃuːt/
soldier /ˈsəʊldʒə/
storm /stɔːm/
terrible /ˈterəbl/
wagon /ˈwægən/
wave (n) /weɪv/

Lesson 24

biography /baɪˈɒgrəfi/
born /bɔːn/
coast /kəʊst/
competition /ˌkɒmpəˈtɪʃn/
conversation /ˌkɒnvəˈseɪʃn/
Czech Republic /ˈtʃek rɪˌpʌblɪk/
guitar /gɪˈtɑː/
Kenya /ˈkenjə/
life /laɪf/
nursery school /ˈnɜːsri ˌskuːl/
operation /ˌɒpəˈreɪʃn/
primary school /ˈpraɪ məri ˌskuːl/
secondary school /ˈsekəndri ˌskuːl//
Swahili /swɑːˈhiːli/
theme park /ˈθiːm ˌpɑːk/

Module 6 – Extra Special

attack /əˈtæk/
building /ˈbɪldɪŋ/
emperor /ˈemprə/
hero /ˈhɪərəʊ/
human /ˈhjuːmən/
law /lɔː/
peace /piːs/
pistol /ˈpɪstl/
pocket /ˈpɒkɪt/
politician /pɒləˈtɪʃn/
president /ˈprezɪdənt/
prison /ˈprɪzn/
prize /praɪz/
rights /raɪts/
temple /ˈtempl/
watch (n) /wɒtʃ/
welcome /ˈwelkəm/

Module 7

Lesson 25

DVD /ˌdiː viː ˈdiː/
next weekend /ˌnekst ˈwiːkend/

paint (v) /peɪnt/
relative /ˈrelətɪv/
this summer /ˌðɪs ˈsʌmə/
tomorrow /təˈmɒrəʊ/
tonight /təˈnaɪt/
Web /web/

Lesson 26

The Bronx /ˌðə ˈbrɒŋks/
cab /kæb/
campsite /ˈkæmpˌsaɪt/
central /ˈsentrəl/
cruise /kruːz/
excited /ɪkˈsaɪtɪd/
harbour /ˈhɑːbə/
lake /leɪk/
musical /ˈmjuːzɪkl/
spend [time] /spend [taɪm]/
stadium /ˈsteɪdiəm/
stay with /ˌsteɪ ˈwɪð/
taxi driver /ˈtæksi ˌdraɪvə/

Lesson 27

difficult /ˈdɪfɪklt/
go-karting /ˈgəʊˌkɑːtɪŋ/
haunted castle /ˈhɔːntɪd ˌkɑːsl/
horse riding /ˈhɔːs ˌraɪdɪŋ/
How about … /ˌhaʊ əˈbaʊt/
idea /aɪˈdɪə/
let's /lets/
picnic /pɪknɪk/
rafting /ˈrɑːftɪŋ/
ride (v) /raɪd/
roller coaster /ˈrəʊlə ˌkəʊstə/
scary /ˈskeəri/
too /tuː/
want /wɒnt/

Lesson 28

activity centre /ækˈtɪvəti ˌsentə/
canoeing /kəˈnuːɪŋ/
crafts /ˈkrɑːfts/
expert /ˈekspɜːt/
instructor /ɪnˈstrʌktə/
lake /leɪk/
packed lunch /ˌpækt lʌntʃ/
rock climbing /ˈrɒk ˌklaɪmɪŋ/
video game /ˈvɪdiəʊ ˌgeɪm/

Module 7 – Extra Special

advertisement /ədˈvɜːtɪsmənt/
deer /dɪə/
lovely /ˈlʌvli/
motorway /ˈməʊtəˌweɪ/

Macmillan Education
Between Towns Road, Oxford OX4 3PP
A division of Macmillan Publishers Limited
Companies and representatives throughout the world

ISBN 978-0-230-53374-5

Text © Colin Granger 2009
Design and illustration © Macmillan Publishers Limited 2009

Original design by Wild Apple Design
Page make-up by Wild Apple Design
Illustrated by Heather Allen; Juliet Breese; Moreno Chiacchiera;
Anna Godwin; Janos Jantner; Gary Joynes; Richard Pashley; Chris
Pavely; Frano Petrusa; Studio Pulsar; Martin Saunders; David Till
Cover design by Designers Collective; background image by iStock

Author's acknowledgements
The author would like to thank Dulcie Booth, Madeleine Williamson,
Mireille Yanow, Victoria Pullin and the rest of the Macmillan editorial
team for their hard work and support.

The publishers would like to thank Magdalena Kondro, Xanthe
Sturt Taylor, Aniela Baranowska, Lidia Domańska, Maria Goretaya,
Beata Goszczyńska, Paulina Grabowska, Dorota Kieszek, Magdalena
Krzyżanowska, Katarzyna Oberda, Anna Petrenkova, Karolina Siupa,
Marta Studniarek, Małgorzata Szpakowska, Renata Szwaj and Ewa
Wódkowska.

The authors and publishers would like to thank the following for
permission to reproduce their photographic materials:
Alamy/ AA World Travel Library p84 (canoes), Alamy/ Jaubert
Bernard p12 (cr), Alamy/ blickwinkel p12 (tr), Alamy/ Tibor Bognar
p60 (b), Alamy/ Jason Horowitz p36 (tl), Alamy/ i4images premium
p10 (keyboard), Alamy/ Interfoto Pressebildagentur p53 (harp),
Alamy/Jeff Morgan Tourism & Leisure p84 (climbing), Alamy/ Jupiter
Images p78 (e), Alamy/ Willy Matheisl p48 (t), Alamy/ Motoring
Picture Library p65 (Ferrari), Alamy/ Andrew Paterson p40 (c),
Alamy/ PhotoDreams p78 (g), Alamy/ Howard Taylor p24 (tr), Alamy/
Travelshots.com p60 (d), Alamy/ Julie Woodhouse p89 (br);
Bananastock pp9 (b, brown, black, grey, brown eye), 12 (ct), 17 (bl),
30 (tr), 37 (baby), 40 (a), 72 (tr), 78 (h), 86;
Brand X pp17 (c), 34 (horse, cobra, ant, camel, buffalo), 37 (gift), 40
(d), 60 (e);
Bridgeman Art Library/ Louvre Paris p54 (Mona Lisa), 61 (a);
ComStock pp9 (wavy), 37 (sofa), 40 (b, f, g);
Corbis pp28 (ball), 37 (clown, rose), 44 (tl), 52 (snowboard, hockey
stick), 53 (football, table tennis, baseball, golf ball, tennis ball), 61
(c, d), Corbis/ Documentary Standard RM p10 (Shetlands, New
Zealand), Corbis/ Edge Value RM p65 (limo), Corbis/ Ted Spiegel p77
(bl), Corbis/ Zefa Value p29 (cr);

Digital Stock pp16 (bl, tr), 65 (New York), 86 (b), Digital Stock/ Corbis
p61 (b);
Digital Vision pp9 (green eye), 34 (cheetah, scorpion, bear);
Getty/ AFP p44 (br), Getty/ Chris Cole p72 (tr), Getty/ Graeme
Cornwallis p84 (loch), Getty/ Michael Goldman p10 (purple), Getty/
Hulton Archive p54 (Pavlova), Getty/ Stephen Johnson p10 (ear),
Getty/ Zigy Kaluzny p78 (c), Getty/ Rob Loud p41 (tr), Getty/ Juergen
Stein p44 (tr), Getty/ Stephen Marks p12 (tl), Getty/ Time Life
Pictures p55 (Picasso), Getty/ Yellow Dog Productions p12 (cb);
Image Source pp9 (straight), 16 (tl), 40 (e), 53 (highjump);
John Foxx Images p34 (snail, fly, owl, horse);
Jupiterimages pp 78 (a), 86, Jupiterimages/ Roger Charity pp12 (tl),
84 (pottery), Jupiterimages/ Kay Chermush p44 (bl), Jupiterimages/
Carlos Domingues p51 (br), Jupiterimages/ Christina Fallara p36 (br),
Jupiterimages/ Corrie McCluskey p77 (br);
Macmillan Publishers LTD/ Paul Bricknell p65 (dinosaur), Macmillan
Publishers LTD/ Dean Ryan/Rob Judges p52 (racquet), Macmillan
Publishers LTD/ David Tolley pp28 (pen), 37 (chocolate),
Mary Evans Picture Library/ p54 (Curies);
NASA/ p16 (c);
Natural History Museum, London p60 (c);
Nature Photo Library/ Kim Taylor p34 (mosquito);
Pathfinder p85 (tr);
PA Photos p52 (tr);
Photoalto p10 (carrots, steak);
Photodisc/ pp9 (curly), 12 (bl, br), 25 (tl), 34 (tortoise, deer, dog,
mouse, chimp, elephant), 42 (tr), 60 (tr);
Powerstock p34 (dolphin);
Punchstock / Brand X p39, Punchstock/ Image Source pp10 (park),
78 (d), 86 (t), Punchstock/ ThinkStock pp78 (b), 86;
Rex Features/ Action Press p77 (tr), Rex Features/ Peter Brooker p60
(a), Rex Features/ Everett Collection p62 (br), Rex Features/ Aimo-
Koivisto p37 (ride), Rex Features/ Sara Jaye p41 (br), Rex Features/
Nils Jorgensen p52 (fencing helmet), Rex Features/ Martin Lee p24
(br), Rex Features/ C. T. Tavin/Everett p55 (Marx Bros), Rex Features/
Ian Waldie p65 (Beckham);
Robert Harding/ Amanda Hall p12 (t);
Stockbyte pp9 (red), 10 (clock, music), 28 (bag), 37 (glasses), 52
(riding hat), 91, 99;
Superstock pp10 (boat), 17 (tl, tr), 52 (br), Superstock/ Sebastian
Gollings p10 (exam), Superstock/ Prisma p78 (f), 86.

Commissioned photography by:
Paul Bricknell pp 7, 10 (Ian, Nyree), 13, 15 (t1, t2, t3), 20, 21, 24 (c),
30 (Nyree), 43, 48 (b), 50, 63, 67, 79, 81.
Dean Ryan pp 23 (1– 6), 27 (1-6), 28 (b,d,f,g,hi), 29 (b), 52 (5), 88 (4).

Printed and bound in Thailand

2013 2012 2011 2010 2009
10 9 8 7 6 5 4 3 2 1